101 Great
Collectibles
for Kids

by Diane L. Oswald

Illustrations by Brent Roderick

Antique Trader Books

A division of Landmark Specialty Publications

ISBN: 0-930625-75-7
Library of Congress Catalog Card Number: 97-72686

Editor: *Allan W. Miller*
Assistant Editor: *Elizabeth Stephan*
Copy Editor: *Sandra Holcombe*
Art Director & Cover Design: *Jaro Sebek*
Production Assistants: *Sabine Beaupré, Barb Brown Loney,*
   Aaron Wilbers

Printed in the United States of America

To order additional copies of this
book or a catalog please contact:

Antique Trader Books
P.O. Box 1050
Dubuque, Iowa 52004
1-800-334-7165

Table of Contents

For our family and friends,
and especially for our children,
Emily, Scott, Katharine, and Jay.

Acknowledgments

·······································

Collectors are a close bunch, and several have contributed to the success of this book through their enthusiasm for the project. We would, however, like to thank the following collectors in particular for sharing their collections and information: Bob Albert, Mike Brenemen, Larry Disney, Joanne Platt, Bradley Cole Swain, and Pamela Cairns.

For their encouragement and support, we gratefully acknowledge Floyd and Alma Maxwell, Linda and Dan Barclay, Harry Oswald, Katharine Lambeth, Jay Lambeth, Peter and Pidge Curtiss, Ann and Eric Voss, Cody Southworth, Lindsay Long, Christopher Barclay, Cameron Barclay, Gary and Melissa Miller, members of Brazos Writers, and members of The Brazos Valley Society of Children's Book Writers and Illustrators. Also, many thanks to our Editor, Allan Miller, Marketing Director, Elizabeth Smith, and our Publisher, Antique Trader Books, for their professionalism and vision for this project. Finally, for unwavering support during the writing and illustration of this work, we thank our wonderful husbands, John Oswald and Ben Roderick.

Diane and Brent

INTRODUCTION

Almost all people, at some point in their lives, have been collectors—whether they knew it or not. Here's a test: Question your friends and family until you find those who claim to have never collected a thing. Then, look in their closets and count the number of T-shirts or baseball caps they've brought back from vacations. Look on their bedroom shelves to see how many knickknacks are on display. If they're music enthusiasts, perhaps they have a tremendous record, tape, or compact disc collection—or, they might have a bunch of books, sports cards, photographs, refrigerator magnets, videos, post cards, or just about anything else that interests or entertains them. Chances are at least some type of collection has taken root.

People collect what they like. Some collectors have a few treasures that are kept for sentimental reasons, while others have rooms full of collectibles they would never part with. It can be surprising to discover what's become "collectible." Old cereal boxes, salt and pepper shakers, comic books, and paper weights are highly sought after, and there are many other popular collecting categories.

Collectors choose *what* to collect for many different reasons, but the reasons *to* collect are similar. Collecting is fun! It's a great way to meet others who share similar interests, to learn about something new, and collecting provides a sense of purpose. A collection is the domain of its collector and it reflects the collector's interests, personality, and efforts. Just like collectors themselves, no two collections are exactly alike.

Take your own collection for example. No matter what you collect, your collection will be "one of a kind." Even if you and a friend both collect movies, the ones that each of you select will be somewhat different. Similarly, if you and another friend both collect seashells, the kinds and shapes of the shells will vary quite a bit.

Some people collect a particular item because they think it might increase in value. What may begin as a collection becomes more of a business and less of a hobby. While investment collecting has its place, this book is not concerned with the value or potential value of collectibles. Many things, including age, condition, and rarity contribute to the value of a collectible, but collecting should, first and foremost, be fun. While some values are provided in this book, they are only intended to give a general idea of a collectible's affordablity.

Many of the 101 collectibles in this book can be found in new, antique, or used condition. As you might expect, collectibles in new or antique condition may be priced quite high; however, if you are willing to scour garage sales, church bazaars, and auctions, each collectible in this book can be found for under $10. Keep in mind though, that there may come a point when you decide to buy expensive collectibles.

As your collection matures, you might want to spend more money on individual pieces to improve the quality of your collection. The frayed edges of a favorite comic book or the worn paint on an old toy may send you in search of a better example of the same thing—or maybe you'll decide that you *really* want an early Barbie Doll, antique button, or historical autograph for your collection. The great news is that collecting is one hobby that can grow with you and your budget!

Collect what you can now and, as you are able, trade up to improve the quality and variety in your collection. There's a real sense of accomplishment and pride as you see your collection mature. As that happens, you will no doubt meet people who share your interests, and who may be able to help you aquire additional collectibles.

This book is full of suggestions on what to collect, how to get started, and how to display your collection. Most of the collectibles can be found almost anywhere, many of them costing a few dollars or less. While I hope you're impressed with the number of collectibles included in this book, they're only the tip of the iceberg. There's an endless number of collectibles for you to discover throughout your lifetime, so make sure you collect what you like, and enjoy what you collect!

How to Use this Book

At this point, you might be asking "What makes these 101 collectibles so great anyway?" Well, first, we've compiled a variety of collectibles that should appeal to a broad range of interests. Regardless of your age, experiences, or where you live, you should be able to find something of interest. Not everyone will agree that bells, boxes, or business cards are great collectibles, but it's almost certain that someone will.

Second, none of the 101 collectibles in this book are trendy. This means that they should be around from year to year to keep your collection growing. You should be able to find most of them almost anywhere.

Third, each collectible has a story to tell. The story includes information about its inventor, why it was developed, the impact it made on society, and more. We've tried to provide a glimpse of the story behind each of the 101 collectibles in this book, but more can be learned if you're willing to ask questions and do some homework.

This book is rather unique among children's literature. It was not written to be read from cover to cover. Instead, it was designed to whet the appetites of aspiring collectors. Flipping through or scanning the pages is normal, and encouraged! For this reason, the entries are brief and informative, the pictures are brilliantly colored and drawn with a dash of whimsy, and we've thrown in a few "extras" to keep it interesting. Whenever possible, a bit of history, a relevant quotation, and a list of related collectibles has been provided.

Use this book as a compass for your collecting journey. Browse, look at the pictures, scan the quotes, and whenever a particular collectible strikes your fancy—read the entire entry. Most of all, let this be an idea book, not only for what to collect, but also for where to look, how to display, and how to find out more about your collectibles.

Collecting, and learning about your collection, can be a life-long pursuit filled with new friends, great buys, and wonderful displays. You might begin collecting one thing and end up with a collection of something entirely different, but that's OK. It's *your* journey, and you get to decide where it's going to take you!

Getting Started

There was a time when a collector was someone who collected stamps, coins, or rocks. Today, almost anything can be a collectible—and, while most collections are groups of related items, some are an assortment of things the collector just happens to like. Collecting is one of the most unrestricted hobbies in the universe. In fact, there's only one rule of collecting we must all live by.

We can only collect things that we buy, that are given to us, or that we find in nature—if there are no laws against taking them home. Too many collectors of all ages have been injured or arrested by breaking this rule. People have been cut and scratched while sneaking snips of old barbed wire fences for their collections. Some people have even been prosecuted for taking cups, plates, and menus from restaurants. Always respect other people's property and ask permission before taking anything. Also, take time to consider a few other things before deciding what to collect.

One of the most important things to think about is what interests you. What are your favorite subjects in school? Do you like science, mathematics, history, music, or art? How do you spend your time after school? Do you cook, listen to music, play sports, or watch movies? Is there something you've always wanted to learn about? How about antiques, books, gardening, or camping? Answer these questions, and you might have a starting point. Clues to what we might enjoy collecting are often sprinkled throughout our activities.

Once you think of a few options, then you must consider availability. For example, if you live in Ithaca, New York, and neither you nor your family ever leave the state, then collecting seashells might be difficult. By the same token, if you live in Boston, Massachusetts, it may take a while to build up a collection of barbed wire. Choose, then, a collectible that is reasonably available where you live.

Also, can you afford the type of collectibles that you are considering? If you get $2 a week for allowance, it might take an entire year of saving to buy a gold antique thimble. In that case, it might make more sense to start collecting modern thimbles. If you know that you won't have any money at all to spend, though, focus on one of the many "free" collectibles listed in this book. Used newspapers, magazines, or stamps torn from envelopes mailed to your house are all collectibles you can find at no cost.

Where are you going to keep your collection? If it's going to be in your bedroom, how much room will you have? Will you have to add shelves or drawers to display it? There might not be enough space for a collection of 100 lunch boxes if you live in a small apartment, but you can probably find enough room to keep a collection of postcards. It's important to consider where and how to display your collectibles before you get started.

If you collect posters, you will need permission and space to hang them on the wall. If you collect stamps, a stamp album is best, but a shoe box will work. Think about how you might arrange your collectibles before deciding what to collect.

Displaying your treasures is half the fun and half the work of collecting. Look at how others display their collections. Don't be afraid to ask friends, family, and even dealers for ideas. Look at store and museum exhibits and incorporate any of the techniques you like. Most of all, use your imagination and all of the props you can find. While there are many commercial display racks, shelves, and frames, a little ingenuity can work, too. Chicken wire, barn wood, cinder blocks, and hangers can sometimes be fashioned into functional and appealing displays. Ask your parents to give you a hand, and see what you can come up with.

Once you decide what to collect, where to keep the collection, and how to display it, consider how you will keep it organized. Many collections are eventually sold or thrown away because they grew out of control. When a collection is piled in boxes, stuffed in drawers, or packed on shelves, it isn't much fun to look at. The best collections are organized.

Take the time to arrange your collectibles in some logical order, and, each time you add a piece to your collection, write down the manufacturer's name and the date that it was made. Using one of the methods listed in the chapter titled "Inventory Options," you might want to include other pertinent information such as where you got it, what it cost, and so on. Keeping this kind of information about your collectibles is a great way to learn, and it makes sharing and trading with other collectors easier and more fun.

Finally, will you be able to take care of the collection? If you collect plants, will you remember to water them? If you collect silver spoons, will you polish them? Taking care of a collection may not be as much fun as assembling it, but it's just as important.

As your collection grows, there will be other things to think about. Should you buy more than one of the same thing? Is it a good idea to join a collectors group? Should you trade or sell some of the items in your collection to get better ones? How many collectibles are enough? As you flip through the pages in this book, think about these questions and try to answer them. Considering the options is all part of the collector's journey—and, if you're lucky, you'll answer them with a great collection that grows just large enough!

Get started now. Browse these pages, enjoy the pictures, and happy collecting!

A Note to Parents and Grandparents

Congratulations! Those special children in your life just took a greater interest in the world, by becoming collectors. Whether your children or grandchildren collect marbles, books, insects, games, post cards, or any one of the other endless possibilities, they'll probably make friends, learn new things, and have a great deal of fun in the process. All your children need is your support.

This new endeavor might mean taking them to beaches where they can look for shells, letting them browse at used book sales, or helping them learn how to take pictures. Regardless of what they decide to collect, it should provide more opportunities to spend time together. Enjoy this special time, but realize that there may be a few bumps along the way.

As the parent of two children who bring bottle caps, turtles, feathers, acorns, rocks, sand, and icicles into the house proclaiming, "This is my new collection," I've had my share of bumps—but, through trial and error, I've developed some guidelines which make it easier to survive children's collecting quests. I share them with you, in the hope that your ride will be easier than mine!

1. Never tell children what to collect: A collection is a very personal thing, reflecting the interests, efforts, and personality of the collector. It is one of the few areas where children can, and should, have a great deal of control, so, if necessary, bite your tongue, cover your mouth, or go outside and scream, but never tell children what *to* collect. Naturally, for reasons of safety, expense, space, or your beliefs, it may be necessary sometimes to tell children what they can *not* collect.

2. Set limits: While it isn't good to tell children what to collect, it is important to set limits. Let young collectors know how much space a collection can take up; how much money can be spent; whether or not you consider animals to be collectibles; and how much time can be devoted to finding, organizing, and researching collectibles so it won't interfere with homework or chores.

3. Support your children's interests: Work with them to create storage and display space. For birthdays or other holidays, give books that will help them learn about their collectibles. If possible, support your children's hobbies financially by providing a reasonable allowance and taking them in search of collectibles. This might mean Saturday treks to garage sales, flea markets, auctions, parks, beaches, or wherever their collectibles are found.

4. Show interest—but not too much: Collecting should be the collectors' domain, where they can make decisions and learn about their collections independently. Enjoy the time together searching for collectibles, setting up display space, and listening as they tell you about their hobbies, but don't direct their collecting efforts. If an over zealous adult takes over by adding to, re-organizing, or managing the collecting process, it may cease to be fun for young collectors.

5. Allow children's collections to open up opportunities for teaching: Almost every collection can be related to an educational outing. Trips to a museum, library, national park, or zoo can almost always in some way be related to children's collections. If your youngsters have collections of coffee mugs, take them to a factory or museum where they can learn about the manufacturing process. If your children collect rocks, a visit to a national park, if only to look at the rocks and formations, should be met with enthusiasm.

Use your imagination to help increase your collectors' knowledge and enjoyment without interfering. Who knows? If you spend enough time supporting your young collectors' quests, you might even become a collector yourself!

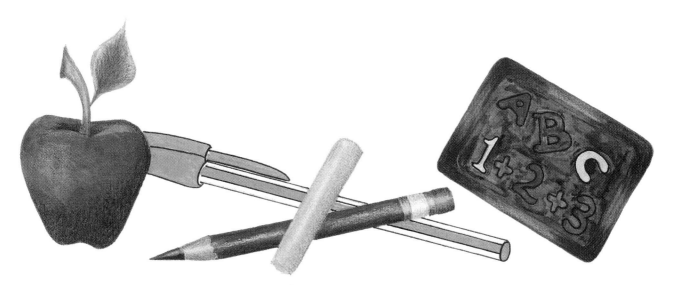

A NOTE TO TEACHERS AND YOUTH LEADERS

Collecting is a positive activity that can be both educational and fun. The 101 collectibles covered in this book don't even scratch the surface of possibilities. Adding a section to your curriculum, or dedicating a troop meeting, might encourage students or scouts to begin their own collections. Collecting almost anything can open up new opportunities to make learning fun!

Art, history, science, and sociology are but a few of the subjects that can be addressed by incorporating collecting into your curriculum or program. For example, students who collect T-shirts can learn about the art of silk-screening, the history of invention (i.e., the T-shirt was designed for sailors in the U.S. Navy in 1942), the science of synthetic fabrics, or the sociology of communicating through clothing. Using T-shirts, or almost any other collectible as a springboard, you can incorporate children's personal interests into your curriculum, and, thereby, hold their attention by making them feel more involved.

Use your imagination, and there's no telling how many ways you can think of to include collecting in your teaching or program. To help you get started, here are six exercises that you might want to consider. The first three activities are geared towards younger children, while the remaining ones are suitable for children in the fourth grade and higher. Although these activities were written with students in mind, they can be adapted for other youth groups including pre-school, scouts, and even Sunday school classes.

#1

Ask the students to bring something from their own collections for show and tell. Let them talk about why they became interested in their particular collectibles, how they got started, and other details about their collections. If students want to participate, but have not yet started collections of their own, ask them to talk about something that they hope to collect. Perhaps they can bring in pictures of their future collectibles.

#2

Ask the students to bring in one collectible for the "classroom collection." This collectible can be brought from home or collected on a field trip. To help them focus their efforts you can:
1. Name specific collectibles, such as postcards, seashells, or books.
2. Ask the students to bring in the most interesting collectibles they can find.
3. Ask the students to bring in specific examples of something (i.e., old technology, artistic expression, or genius).

The "classroom collection" can be put on display, passed around, or used as the basis for one of the other activities mentioned in this chapter.

#3

Ask the students to bring in a variety of old magazines. When there are enough magazines covering a variety of subjects, have them make individual "collage collections" from pictures of what they would like to collect.

#4

Divide the students into small groups. Make copies of the Table of Contents in this book. Ask the students to brainstorm and come up with a list of their own. Then, have each group share the five most unique collectibles from their list with the rest of the class.

#5

Divide the students into small groups. List five man-made collectibles on the chalkboard and let each group select one collectible in turn. Then, instruct the groups to brainstorm to come up with at least five inventions that made their particular collectible possible. For example, if jewelry was one of the collectibles chosen, then string, clasps, beads, chains, and plastics might be mentioned as a few things that made jewelry possible. Please note that the more complex the collectible, the easier it will be for students to answer the question.

#6

Ask the students to write a paper on their collection, or on what they would like to collect. The paper can cover the history, use, or design of a particular collectible; why they enjoy collecting; how they got started; how they found their favorite collectible; or any other aspect of their collection or the collecting process.

There are many ways to incorporate collecting into your curriculum or program. You'll probably find, too, that collecting can serve as a fresh, new approach to getting students and scouts more involved, both inside the classroom and out!

INVENTORY OPTIONS

A great collection is ordered in some logical fashion, displayed well, and inventoried. An inventory is just a list of something with any details that are of interest to the person making it. An inventory can help you manage your collection by keeping track of its contents. For example, if you collect dolls, an inventory can tell you who manufactured a particular doll, the age or date that it was made, who you bought it from, what the asking price was, how much you actually paid, what condition it was in, and any other information that you may want to know later. All of this information can help you make decisions about your collection.

An inventory can help you decide what to add next, how much to buy or sell a collectible for, and whether or not you really want to make a trade. The trick is to keep enough information to answer most of the questions that come up in the future. Depending upon how detailed you want to be, there are a number of ways to keep this information.

You can keep a hand-written, photographic, or computer-based inventory. Each of these options have certain, distinct advantages you should consider before deciding which one is best for you.

1. Hand-written

Many collectors keep a hand-written list of everything that is in their collection. Index cards work well, as do sheets of paper stored in a loose-leaf notebook. Using a format similar to the one below, you might want to list the following information for each of your collectibles:

Collectible Name or Description_____

Manufacturer's Name_____   Date Made_____

Color_____   Size_____   Price Paid_____

There are many advantages to keeping a written inventory. For example, since a written inventory travels better than one stored on a computer, you can easily take index cards or a notebook on collecting trips and add information as you go. Also, keeping a written inventory is less expensive than buying special software or film. Finally, it might just be that for you, it's easier to inventory your collection by hand.

2. Photographs or Video

Many collectors take pictures of their collection. This allows them to easily share their collection with others, and to document what they have in case anything is ever lost or stolen. While this can be an expensive option, it's worth considering if you enjoy taking pictures or if your collection is particularly valuable. Also, video recorders are sometimes used to document or inventory a collection, but this is more for fun, or for insurance purposes. Some collectors combine photographs with a written or computer inventory to keep track of the details.

3. Computer

If you have a computer and know how to use it, there are several software options available to you. There are a few software packages which have been specifically designed to help you manage your collection. These packages allow you to enter many different data fields for each collectible. Some basic functions that you'll want are: sorting, searching, and adding or updating collectibles. Some of these packages even allow you to generate special reports detailing prices or your "wish list."

Two companies that produce software for collectors are: The Third Rail, 3377 Cimarron Drive, San Ynez, CA 93460, (805) 688-7370 and Noodleware Software Company, P.O. Box 83-CTM, Lindenhurst, NY 11757-0083, (516) 321-9776. Other software companies that produce collecting programs may be found in collector's magazines.

It's possible that your parents might even have a program that you can use. Some collectors use home inventory software to keep track of their collectibles. While not specifically designed for collections, home inventory software does have fields for the model number, manufacturer, and value of your home furnishings or collectibles.

Finally, there are a large number of databases that can be used to keep an inventory. If either you or your parents have a database program, then you can create a special database to track just the fields that you are interested in. A simple database might contain the manufacturer's name, the date the collectible was made, the size, the color, and the price paid. A more elaborate database may include fifteen or more fields relating to the inventor, patent date, or design of each collectible.

While databases are one of the most flexible options, they are also the most difficult to learn. If either of your parents are familiar with the database software, then perhaps they can help you set up a custom collection database. Once the database forms have been designed, data entry and running reports can easily be learned.

How you decide to inventory your collection is entirely up to you; however, it is easier to keep an inventory from the very beginning, than to go back and create one for a growing collection. Consider the advantages of keeping an inventory, as well as the costs, to determine if it's right for you and your collection.

What's Next

Once you begin collecting, you may want to meet others with similar interests. Sharing information and trading with other collectors is fun, and it can help you learn about your collection.

Most collectors love their hobby and are more than willing to share information and talk with new collectors. Some collectors even collect two or more of the same thing so that they will have something to trade. You can meet these people by chance wherever you find your collectibles, or through organized clubs.

There are many collecting groups made up of people who share similar interests. There are groups for people who collect spoons, stamps, penny banks, and many other things. Some of these groups have branches that meet locally, while others keep in touch with members through newsletters or magazines. Also, many of these clubs have annual meetings where members can gather to exchange information, hear speakers, and trade amongst themselves. You can find out about specific collectors and collecting groups through various antiques and collectibles magazines or through a directory such as *Maloney's Antiques & Collectibles Resource Directory*, (Antique Trader Books). If you buy collectibles from specialty stores or dealers, don't overlook them as a resource. They can provide interesting information and help you to find other collectors. Meeting collectors and dealers is a great way to learn about your hobby—but it's not the only way.

Your local library, undoubtedly, has or can get books on inter-library loan that include a wealth of information on your collectibles. While you don't have to become an expert to enjoy your collection, you do have the opportunity to become one. You might even discover that the more you learn about your collection, the more you enjoy it. You never know—maybe someday you'll end up writing a book or making a living using the expertise you gain from collecting.

Finally, if you ever get to the point with your collection where you believe it can grow no further, consider related collectibles. Many collectors start out collecting one thing and wind up collecting something else. For example, if, after collecting 500 T-shirts, you decide that your collection has grown too large to continue, why not collect baseball caps for a change of pace? Both of these collectibles can be worn, they are relatively inexpensive, and they cover a wide variety of subjects and designs. Or, if you truly believe that you have collected all of the yo-yos known to man, then collect tops or some other spinning toy. Just keep your eyes open and you will discover many collecting opportunities.

The great thing about collecting is that you always get back more than what you put into it, so make friends, learn, and have a great time!

Advertisements

*"You can tell the ideals of a nation
by its advertisements."*
Norman Douglas, 1868-1952

Look around you. We are surrounded by advertising. Print ads including billboards, display ads in magazines and newspapers, signs, direct mail pieces, and even logos on our toys, clothing, and household goods are everywhere. Do you know what that means? It means that advertising is a great collectible! It has also been around much longer than you might think.

In 1480, an Englishman named William Caxton posted a notice which is believed to be the first "advertisement." Caxton's notice paved the way for the many different forms of advertising that followed. Within a short period of time, posters, handbills, signs, and other printed advertisements became the persuasive, informative, and educational forums of their time. Today, colorful packaging, premiums, direct mail, magazine and newspaper ads, and more offer a smorgasbord of advertising collectibles.

Advertising's purpose has always been to sell products and services, to rally people together for a common cause, or to inform the public—and advertising says a lot about the time when it first appeared. Look at the hair styles, clothing, language and other aspects of the advertisement to get a glimpse of another era. For example, a 1950s store display for the Slinky shows a young boy rocking the famous toy from one hand to another. The slogan reads "The Action-Toy Everyone Knows and Loves to Play With." While the boy's hairstyle could pass for today's fashion, no one in this high-tech, action-oriented toy market would view the Slinky as an "Action-Toy." This ad documents a change in our way of thinking. Forty years ago, a toy that simply moved was considered an "action toy." Today, action toys are superheros, mutants, or villainous figures that live in the pages of our comic books or cartoons. This is only one example, though. Many other changes can be traced through advertising as well.

Old advertisements printed with the names of businesses that no longer exist, telephone numbers beginning with letters in the exchange, instead of numbers, or the company address shown without the ZIP Code, are but a few examples of the changes which can be tracked through advertising. These changes make collecting advertisements fun and they show up in almost every kind of print ad.

Early magazine ads, trading cards, signs, and packaging provide great insight into the past, and they are very popular with today's collectors. Examples of old advertising can be found at antique shows, auctions, flea markets, and occasionally at garage sales or church bazaars. Since some of these items can be quite expensive, how-

15

ever, you might want to begin with the many "free" advertising collectibles that are available.

Pens, drinking glasses, coffee mugs, coasters, and other promotional items are given away by many different kinds of businesses. They are stuffed into product boxes, awarded to customers for their loyalty, and offered as premiums for specific purchases. These no-cost collectibles can help to build your collection at a rapid pace.

The great thing about advertising is that it's very easy to find. Walk down any grocery store isle and see how many packages are printed with special offers for free or low-cost toys, cups, towels, or other items. Look on the back of your favorite cereal, cookies, or chips and you'll probably find an offer or two. Ask your parents if you can have some of their magazines, the packages from household products, or the key chain and cup from the local bank. There are so many options, you might want to specialize in one particular type of advertising collectible.

Specialize by collecting pencils, key chains, car ads, or fruit labels, to help focus your efforts. As your collection grows, you might even want to become more selective, including only unique or antique advertising. Even some of the old advertising pieces are priced at $10 or less.

Antique shows, auctions, and flea markets frequently have old signs, packages, and other promotional items for sale. Even garage sales and church bazaars have been known to supply advertising collectors with some real treasures. Advertising collectibles are perhaps the easiest of all collectibles to find, and they display well in almost any room.

So, why not get started? There are thousands of different advertising collectibles just waiting for you!

Related Collectibles: sales catalogues, labels

Animal Figures

*"I think I could turn and live with animals, they are so placid
and self-contain'd, I stand and look at them long and long."*
Walt Whitman, 1819-1892

Since the days when cave dwellers painted pictures of ancient animals on their walls, man has been fascinated with the wild kingdom. From alligators to wombats, birds to reptiles, the domestic to the exotic—we love animals!

When we can't be with them, we chisel, carve and shape animal figures to display on our tables and shelves. Collecting animal figures can add new excitement to our love and appreciation for our four-footed, winged, finned, crawling, or creeping animal friends, and, for the young collector, the options are almost unlimited.

A collection of animal figures can be narrow in its focus and include only penguins, piranhas, porcupines, or pigs—or it can be broad enough to include any farm, forest, aquatic, or desert animals. Your collection can include only animals found in a particular state, country, or on a certain continent. There are many ways to specialize when collecting animal figures.

Perhaps you prefer to specialize in animal figures that are made from a specific material. For example, many figures are made out of

glass, wood, porcelain, or stone. A wonderful collection of animal figures can be assembled by specializing in figures crafted from any of these materials. Once you decide what kind of animal figures to collect, you can begin the hunt!

Garage sales, flea markets, and retail stores are among the most likely places for you to begin your animal figure collection. The cost of figures will vary depending upon the age, material that they are made of, and who made them. Antique figures, those made from precious metals, or those crafted by well-known artists can be very expensive, but the good news is that most animal figures are reasonably priced, costing as little as $5. As your collection begins to multiply, you will need to think about how to display it.

For a traditional display, set your animal figures on shelves, tables, or in cupboards, or you can bring branches, straw, rocks, or leaves inside to create a more natural looking exhibit. Arrange these natural props to create a prairie, mountain, forest, or other habitat. Place your animals in their correct habitat, and you will have a unique display that will be enjoyed by many.

The options for collecting animal figures are many. One thing is certain, though—unlike their counterparts, animal figures never need to be walked!

Related Collectibles: stuffed animals, photos or drawings of animals

Autographs

....

*"The celebrity is a person who is known
for his well-knownness."*

Daniel Joseph Boorstin, 1914

There are more than 200,000 autograph collectors world-wide, so if you decide to join them, you'll be in good company. Nearly 20,000 new collectors take up "Philography" or the "Love of Writing" each year. Many of these collectors are searching for the signatures of movie stars, sports heroes, and politicians; however, the autographs of famous writers, scientists, musicians and historical figures, are also highly sought after.

Before you can begin, you have to decide what kind of autographs to collect. For the avid football fan or movie buff, the decision might be simple. Whose autographs would you like to have? Are you interested in television actors, authors, musicians, or politicians? The choice is up to you, but once you decide, you have to figure out how you can get the autographs that you want.

There are two basic ways to collect autographs. Autographs can either be provided by a celebrity upon request, or they can be purchased or acquired from someone else. Both of these strategies can lead to a fine autograph collection; however, it is probably more fun to get a personalized autograph than to buy one from someone else.

Many celebrities will provide fans with autographs at concerts, book signings, or sporting events. Some celebrities will even provide autographs through the mail if the request includes a self-addressed stamped envelope. Try writing to the celebrity if you have the address, or to his publisher, agent, fan club, or recording label. The important thing to remember when you request an autograph, is to ask politely and be gracious—whether or not your request is granted. Sending a picture of yourself can be a good strategy since many celebrities are interested in their young fans.

Another way to begin a collection is to buy the autographs you want. There are many dealers who specialize in autographs. They sell their merchandise at antique shows, flea markets, auctions, and through mail-order, and dealers often have a wide variety of autographs ranging in price from $10 to $1,000 or more. The value of an autograph depends upon who the celebrity is, the condition of the signature and the age of the autograph. For example, the signatures of many modern celebrities sell for $25 or less; however, historical photographs can be much more expensive. A photograph signed by Wilbur and Orville Wright sold a few years ago for $10,000.

Another factor in determining the value of an autograph is what it is written on. Cards, autograph albums, T-shirts, baseballs, or other objects that can easily be carried are often presented for celebrities to sign. Sometimes, a celebrity will even carry a supply of photographs to be signed for fans. These are often the only ways a collector can get a personalized autograph. While these autographs may mean the most to collectors, they may not be the most valuable.

Historical photographs, documents, and typed letters with original signatures tend to be the most expensive autographs, and are usually only available through dealers or other collectors. The most valuable autographs, which are difficult to find, are found at the bottom of hand-written, personal letters. Regardless of how expensive each autograph in your collection is, though, you will want to display them.

Autographed pictures, letters, and other documents can either be kept in a photograph album or framed and hung on the wall. Other objects such as baseballs, hats, or books, are nicely displayed on tables and shelves.

Collecting autographs is a fun way to capture and keep a little bit of fame, so if you think that you'll enjoy collecting autographs, start looking for celebrities who have signed on the dotted line, photograph, baseball, or letter. In no time at all, you may discover that autograph collecting is write on!

Related Collectibles: pictures, news clippings, or the work of celebrities

Automotive Collectibles

....

"Did ye not hear it? – No! 'twas but the wind,
Or the car rattling o'er the stony street."
Lord Byron, 1788-1824

The first motorized vehicle was invented by Oliver Evans in 1804. The city of Philadelphia hired Evans to build a machine that could dredge the Schuylkill River and clean the city docks. Evan's five-horsepower, steam-driven vehicle weighed 15-1/2 tons and measured 12 feet wide by 30 feet long. This "Automobile" was driven one and a half miles from its original garage, through downtown Philadelphia to the work area along the river. Despite the success of Evan's steam-powered vehicle, it took another ninety-nine years before the motor-car really took off.

On May 23, 1903, H. Nelson Jackson and Sewell K. Crocker left San Francisco to become the first drivers to complete a coast-to-coast trip by car. On July 26, Jackson and Crocker's twenty-horsepower Winton car pulled into New York City. Ever since this historical trip, Americans have been fascinated by the power and style of the car. Today, a wide variety of automotive collectibles can put you on the road to a great collection!

One of the best automotive collectibles is printed advertisements featuring cars and related products. Old issues of *National Geographic*, *Life*, or other magazines are often the most available and best sources for ads that chronicle the over 5,000 makes and models of cars that have been manufactured. Through advertising, you can track the changing styles and designs of cars over time, and printed advertisements featuring cars are easy to find.

Many "Friends of the Library" book sales around the country offer used magazines dating as far back as the 1960s for little or no money, and dealers at flea markets and antique shows sell magazines and individual ads which date back to the early 1900s. These vintage auto ads have pictures and details about the early models.

Other great sources of pictures and information on cars are old owners' and repair

manuals, dealer brochures, and the many hundreds of books that have been written on cars and their makers. If you want to collect something a little closer to the real thing, though, license plates are worth considering.

License plates are more interesting than most people realize. The letters on a license plate can tell you a great deal about the car that it was issued for. Was the car a city, state, or federal government vehicle? What state was the car registered in? Was it a special use vehicle such as a rental car, delivery truck, or tractor? What was the occupation of the car's owner? Answers to these questions are actually coded messages on license plates.

For example, Diplomats are issued license plates that are red, white, and blue. Additionally, the letter "D" designates the license plate as being assigned to a Diplomat. The letter "A" marks the license plate of an Assembly member, "C" means that the owner is with a Consul, and "S" identifies the driver as Mission Staff. These are but a few of the little known facts that make collecting license plates so much fun! Although license plates are not usually too expensive, they may be more difficult to find than printed car ads.

Old license plates can be found in your family and friend's garages, at flea markets, auctions, or estate sales; however, the best source for old license plates is probably a friendly wrecking yard that sells used auto parts. If you are lucky enough to wander around the wrecking yard with one of the employees, tracking down license plates can be an exciting scavenger hunt.

While looking for license plates, you might find other automotive collectibles along the way. Hood ornaments, gear shift knobs, spark plugs, metal logo tags featuring the names of the manufacturers or dealers, license plate holders, and hub caps also make wonderful collectibles, and there is no better place to find these than a good wrecking yard!

As your collection grows, you might decide to specialize based upon the age of the collectible, the auto manufacturer, or you might limit your collecting to only cars that are no longer made such as Galaxy, Nash, or Pintos. With automotive collectibles, the only limitations are the space to display them, money to purchase them, and time to enjoy them, so rev up your engines and start collecting!

Related Collectibles: transportation collectibles

Baby Rattles

"Behold the child, by Nature's kindly law,
Pleas'd with a rattle, tickled with a straw."
Alexander Pope, 1688-1744

The rattle's ringing bells, rolling beads, or clanking balls, has pleased babies for centuries. It's likely that when you were a baby, a rattle was the first toy to bring a smile to your face. Perhaps it was a fancy silver-plated teething rattle that had belonged to your grandfather, or maybe it was a modern rattle with wooden rings around a spindle that sounds like two sticks being hit together. If memories of a favorite rattle can still bring a smile to your face, then collecting rattles might just make you giggle.

Baby rattles have been made from wood, plastic, ceramic, metal, glass, and fabric. Among the most highly collectible rattles are the hand-carved or precious metal rattles which were crafted into interesting shapes.

Baby rattles vary more in shape than they do in size. After all, a baby's toy has to be small enough to play with, but large enough to keep the baby from swallowing it. Acorn-shaped bell, globe, dumbbell, teething-ring, sleigh bell, pacifier, and animal rattles are among the most common. Depending upon what material a rattle is made from, the design can be very simple or quite intricate. As with most collectibles, the greater the detail, the more desirable the rattle will be to collectors.

Special interest is being shown in elaborate, Victorian rattles that date from the 1880s. These fine examples of early craftsmanship can be difficult to find and quite costly. Still, young collectors can find attractive, affordable rattles if the know where to look.

Flea markets, thrift stores, garage sales, and antique stores are prime collecting spots for rattles of all designs, ages, and values. Retail stores have an assortment of new rattles ranging in price from $5 and up. As your rattle collection grows, look for interesting ways to display them.

Baby rattles can be displayed with teddy bears, dolls, and other fun collectibles to add some variety. They can be set on shelves, tables, or in cupboards. For something a little different, try making a rattle mobile to hang from the ceiling. Just make sure to display your rattle collection in a safe place.

It's important to keep small children away from the rattles in your collection unless a grown-up has inspected them. If any of the rattles are old, they may not meet today's safety standards.

Whether played with or simply admired, a collection of baby rattles can bring smiles to the faces of all who see it. If baby rattles are of interest to you, then go out and see what's shaking!

Related Collectibles: baby cups, baby spoons, baby bottles

Balls

·····················

"Take me out to the ball game, take me out with the crowd.
Buy me some peanuts and cracker jack, I don't care if I never get back."
Jack Norworth, 1879-1959

The ball is probably the oldest toy. From the first smooth, round rock or gourd tossed into the air, to the latest in high-tech synthetic rubber, balls have been an important part of our recreation and sports, and collecting balls offers much more variety than one might think. Baseball, football, tennis, ping pong, racquetball, soccer, golf, croquet, and many other sports exist because of the game rules that have been written around these spherical toys. Everything from wood, plastic, steel, and rubber have been used to make the balls that we play with. This means that the choices for ball collectors are many.

How about a collection that includes the very best in American sports? A great collection can be assembled by focusing on balls with machine-printed autographs of your favorite sports heroes. Look in retail stores for balls endorsed by Michael Jordon, Reggie Jackson, Arnold Palmer, and other celebrity athletes. In no time at all, you'll have a great ball collection to play with or admire. If you're a "one sport" ball collector, then you can specialize another way.

Specializing in a specific type of ball means collecting many different examples of the same thing. For instance, soccer balls come in full-sized regulation models as well as stuffed, wooden, metal, miniature, ceramic, plastic, and many other versions of the kickable collectible. Pick your favorite sport and look for new balls in sporting goods, department, or specialty stores. Used balls frequently roll into garage sales, church bazaars, and flea markets. To add a little variety, why not pick up some related collectibles?

Cups, posters, postcards, pens, and other objects with balls printed on them can round out your collection, and if you add a tennis racquet, baseball glove, golf club, or other related gear, you will have a much more interesting exhibit.

Ball collections can be displayed on specially designed racks or carts, on shelves, dressers, or tables. The trick to keeping balls from rolling off a flat surface is to either put a towel or other textured surface under them, or set them on a ring. The cardboard rings from masking or packing tape work well to keep large balls such as soccer and basketballs in place. For tennis, baseball, and other small balls, cut 1/2-inch sections from an empty paper towel roll to keep them in place.

Collecting balls is an interesting way to enjoy your favorite sport, and you might just have a ball doing it!

Related Collectibles: bats, clubs, gloves, racquets

7

BANKS

....

*"There are three faithful friends –
an old wife, an old dog, and ready money."*
Benjamin Franklin (1706-1790)

Benjamin Franklin's famous sayings on thrift, which were published in *Poor Richard's Almanac*, are credited with making penny banks popular in the United States. In 1793, when penny banks first arrived in America, young and old alike believed "A penny saved is a penny earned." Saving for tomorrow, became a national past time and penny banks offered a fun and entertaining way to "put something away for a rainy day."

Early pottery and porcelain penny banks were molded into simple shapes, but as time went on, banks made of glass, tin, wood, and cast iron were crafted into more complex shapes including animals, people, buildings, and landmarks. Intricate paintings, carvings, casting, and lithographs, attract collectors to these appealing banks.

Many collectors begin by looking for still banks, which have no moving parts. Piggy, safe, and non-mechanical banks with separate shoots for pennies, nickels, dimes, and quarters, are just a few examples of still banks. When the coins are dropped through the slot, they disappear into the belly of the bank. Most still banks have a removable shield where the money can be safely removed; however, some still banks have to be disassembled in order to get the money out, and a few—particularly plastic banks, must be destroyed in order to make a withdrawal.

Collectors can specialize in single-subject penny banks such as dog, globe, building, or car banks. Also, entire collections can be assembled with banks made out of a particular type of material such as cast iron, tin, or glass. Still banks can be collected as souvenirs of places and events, remembrances of great people, or examples of cartoon art. There are thousands of different styles of still banks, but for even greater variety, consider banks that move.

Mechanical banks, which have moving parts, have been popular since the 1800s. When a coin is deposited in, or a lever pressed on a mechanical bank, some type of action occurs. In the old mechanical banks

an eagle might tip the penny into the slot, Humpty Dumpty might raise the coin in his hand up to his mouth, or a goat might move forward. Most often the action, which was triggered by the coin, helps to deposit the money into the bank. While antique mechanical banks can cost hundreds or even thousands of dollars, there are more affordable options.

Modern mechanical banks include gum machines, slot machine banks, and some coin roll banks. These banks are hand-cranked, electric, or battery-powered, and, at prices of $10 to $20, they are the most affordable moving banks. As you might suspect, new banks of any kind are easier to find than antiques.

New still and mechanical banks are available at most department, toy, gift, and specialty stores. Antique banks can be found at antique stores, flea markets, estate sales, and from other collectors, but—if you decide to collect antique banks—be careful.

Many early banks have been reproduced. These modern versions look so much like the original, that collectors are sometimes tricked into believing that they are old. A dealer might try to sell a reproduction bank for the price of what the original would sell for. This can be a costly error for the unknowing collector. When buying banks secondhand, make sure you know what you're getting. Find a good price guide and a trusted expert to help you become familiar with the styles, sizes, and values of genuine antique banks.

Collecting banks is a fun and interesting hobby. Regardless of what kind you collect, the fun will be in the bank!

Related Collectibles: coin purses and cash boxes

Barbed Wire and Other Cowboy Collectibles

8

*"Last night as I lay on the prairie,
And looked at the stars in the sky,
I wondered if ever a cowboy
would drift to that sweet bye-and-bye."*
The Cowboy's Dream (Anonymous)

The end of the Civil War marked the beginning of the range cattle industry in the United States. Boot-clad cowboys running herds across Texas were among the first to "round them up and head them out." Cowboys fought the pounding heat, thick dust, and the poison of the dreaded rattlesnake to get their herds to market. It was a trip laced with peril as cowboys and their cattle traveled from one watering hole to another, dodging the bullets and arrows of rustlers and Indians. It was a life destined to change with the times.

The cowboy's heyday lasted roughly from about 1866 until railroad tracks replaced the Chisholm Trail as the route to get cattle to market. By 1890, most of the cattle herds had been fenced in, and the round-up and long drive was just a page in the history books. It's the cowboy's rugged trail image, and the charm of the Old West that has captured the interest and imagination of today's collectors. There are a great many collectibles to consider—everything from barbed wire to britches played an important role in the lives of America's cowboys.

Who hasn't seen an old western movie where either the cowboy, a bad guy, or a dim-witted cow gets tangled up in a barbed wire fence? With over

1,000 different types, barbed wire is an honest-to-goodness cowboy collectible, and each style and variation of barbed wire has a name. Harbaugh's Torn Ribbon, Meriwether Snake Wire, and Scutt's Wood Block are but a few of the rough and tumble tags given to the prickly wire.

In the West, it is still possible to find old barbed wire fences in the brush, and although they may be a challenge to find, they offer a time-tested collectible at a great price—often, for free.

First, ask the landowner or park ranger for permission before setting out to find barbed wire. Never cut wire from a standing fence, it is dangerous, and the fence may still be in use. Instead, look for old barbed wire fences that have fallen or have been pulled down. Take a pair of leather gloves, wire cutters, and a heavy canvas bag along on your collecting trip. Put on gloves and then use the wire cutters to snip an 18- to 22-inch piece of wire for your collection.

To avoid accidental scrapes and cuts, keep the barbed wire in the heavy canvass bag until you have a chance to mount it. If you don't live in barbed-wire country, you may have to buy pieces for your collection.

There are a handful of people who specialize in cowboy or western collectibles. These dealers are the most likely to have barbed wire for sale. Usually, barbed wire is sold in strips between 18 and 22 inches in length, many priced at less than $10; however, a single strand of barbed wire can cost over $200 if it is an old, rare pattern. Mounted collections and decorative displays can occasionally be found with prices ranging from $10 and up.

For the purposes of exhibiting your collection, it is best to select pieces of barbed wire that are all the same length. Many collectors nail the strips of barbed wire to a sheet of plywood to display. Others actually mount the wire on a flat board and frame the entire display. Barbed wire can be one of the most affordable cowboy collectibles, but it certainly isn't the only one.

Fencing tools such as barb pliers, wire stretchers, and loppers compliment even the smallest of barbed wire collections, and spurs, gloves, saddles, horseshoes, chaps, lariats, and cowboy hats also help to celebrate the old West and round out a collection. The earliest examples of these collectibles can be quite expensive, but more recent examples can be found at thrift shops, flea markets, garage sales, farm sales, and church bazaars for as little as $5. Toys, posters, shirts, and other modern collectibles with cowboys or images of the Old West printed on them are also affordable.

Whichever direction your cowboy collection grows, just "Go West young collector, go West!"

**Related Collectibles: horse or cow collectibles,
maps of the Old West**

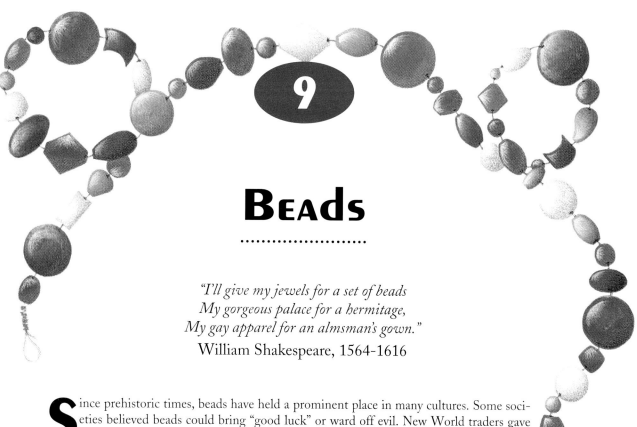

Beads

....

*"I'll give my jewels for a set of beads
My gorgeous palace for a hermitage,
My gay apparel for an almsman's gown."*
William Shakespeare, 1564-1616

Since prehistoric times, beads have held a prominent place in many cultures. Some societies believed beads could bring "good luck" or ward off evil. New World traders gave beads as gifts and used them to barter. Long ago, Native Americans exchanged beads for the things they needed. Beads have been so revered by some, that a single bead was considered a fair trade for an entire beaver pelt which could be used to make warm clothing. In some religions, beads are even used to count prayers.

As early as 4000 B.C., ancient Egypt was a source for finely crafted beads. Clay, stone, glass, and wood are among the earliest materials used in bead making. Even seeds, nuts, and shells have been fashioned into beads and strung together to make necklaces. Today, beads are made of every imaginable material from plastic to gold, and everything in between. And, the number of styles is mind boggling.

Beads come in many different shapes and sizes. Although most beads are round, they can also be flat, egg-shaped, tube-shaped, or cube-shaped. Beads can range in size from a tiny grain of rice up to a large lemon. Also, the variety of colors used to create beads rivals that found in a deluxe box-set of crayons. Special beads with letters, animals or designs painted on them are prized by collectors, and beads with unique glazes or decals are also highly sought after.

New beads are easily found at craft shops and in many department stores. They are sold in packaged containers, by the ounce, or individually. To find old beads, look for jewelry and other beaded items at garage sales, church bazaars, flea markets, and other secondhand sales.

Collectors often have specific projects in mind when they gather beads. Beads are often strung together to make necklaces, earrings, or other jewelry. This makes displaying your collection easy—just wear them, or use beads to decorate other useful items. Purses, throw pillows, jackets, shirts, pants, and shoes can be given new life when adorned with beads. Or, fill a crystal vase, a drinking glass, or a clear bottle with brightly colored beads and set it on a shelf to be admired. Some collectors even drape long strands of beads from the ceiling for room dividers or curtains. As long as your imagination holds out, there is almost no limit to the ways that you can display beads from your collection!

Whether hand-painted or mass-produced, the elegance of a single decorative bead is nothing short of beautiful. Imagine, then, how stunning your entire collection will be!

Related Collectibles: sequins, buttons

10

Bells

....

"Keeping time, time, time,
In a sort of Runic rhyme,
To the tintinnabulation that
so musically wells
From the bells, bells, bells, bells,
Bells, bells, bells."

Edgar Allan Poe, 1809-1849

Since biblical times, bells have sung out the good news of birth, the celebration of weddings, the sorrow of death, the alarm of fire, and the start of community events. Church bells sound on Sunday mornings, carillons play holiday songs, and school bells call the class to order. We rely on door bells to tell us we have company, dinner bells to call us to the table, and jingle bells to alert us to Santa's arrival.

In every corner of the world, bells have been crafted to fill an endless number of needs. Although most large bells are metal, many smaller bells are wood, clay, porcelain, and glass. From the tiny bell hanging on delicate gold necklaces to the massive, 222.56 ton bell at the Kremlin in the former Soviet Union, bells hold a prominent place in our lives and history. It's no wonder, then, that so many people enjoy collecting bells.

With hundreds of different designs, many bell collectors choose to specialize. School, sleigh, farm, cow, and harness bells come in a variety of sizes and styles. Elegant cut glass and brass servant bells, once used to summon the help, can make a beautiful display. Hand-painted porcelain bells depicting famous people, places, or animals are held dear by many collectors, and most cities and states are featured on one or more bells with decaled designs.

The musically inclined might want to collect bells that best approximate the notes in the scale. True tones resonating from the rim of a bell are music to many collectors' ears. Hand-held chimes used by bell choirs can also be collected to orchestrate a musical collection. With these few examples, it's easy to see that the bell collector's options are many and the opportunity is great.

Once you begin collecting bells, you'll find them easy to display. A table, bookshelf, or a china cupboard will make a wonderful home for your bell collection. Just make sure that the display is safe from foot traffic. If a bell, even a metal one, falls to the floor, it can easily be damaged.

Bells can be found almost anywhere. Flea markets, gift shops, and thrift stores are among the best places to look for them. Many small bells are priced at only a dollar or two; however, large or fancy bells can cost $100 or more. Like anything else, if you begin spending large amounts of money, then you should become familiar with the various styles and values. Buy a price guide that has a listing for bells, talk with a knowledgeable collector, and buy only from a trusted dealer.

If you enjoy the sound of a church bell ringing on Sunday morning, then collecting bells just might ring your chimes!

Related Collectibles: gongs and table-top chimes

11

Belt Buckles

·······················

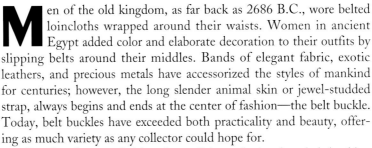

"Bobby Shaftoe's gone to sea,
Silver buckles on his knee;
He'll come back and marry me,
Pretty Bobby Shaftoe."
Anonymous Nursery Rhyme

Men of the old kingdom, as far back as 2686 B.C., wore belted loincloths wrapped around their waists. Women in ancient Egypt added color and elaborate decoration to their outfits by slipping belts around their middles. Bands of elegant fabric, exotic leathers, and precious metals have accessorized the styles of mankind for centuries; however, the long slender animal skin or jewel-studded strap, always begins and ends at the center of fashion—the belt buckle. Today, belt buckles have exceeded both practicality and beauty, offering as much variety as any collector could hope for.

People, places, and things have all been depicted on belt buckles. There are buckles commemorating the United States Bicentennial, the anniversary of the Old Oregon Trail, and thousands of other local and national events. There are cowboy, military, advertising, and a host of other specialty buckles.

Belt buckles are often awarded as prizes to the best trap shooter, the sportsman who catches the largest fish, the bowler with the highest score, or for other great achievements. The Elks, Boy Scouts, Lions Club, and many other fraternal and service organizations have had belt buckles specifically designed for their organizations. Policemen, firemen, and railroad men have, over the years, worn many styles of buckles depicting their vocations.

Nickel-plated, brass, and cast metal are among the most common materials used in buckle making, but plastic, wood, and ivory have also been used. The variety of subjects depicted on belt buckles is mind-boggling. To get a little direction on where to start, you might want to take an interest inventory.

What are your hobbies? What sports do you play? Do you know what you want to be when you grow up? Does your father belong to any organizations that you particularly like? Do either of your parents belong to a service organization that you are interested in? Would you enjoy collecting prize, cowboy, or advertisement buckles? Have you seen any buckles that you might like to have? Ask yourself these questions, think about your other interests, and begin looking for buckles wherever you go.

Belt buckles are relatively common, making them easy to collect. Department, gift, and specialty stores are likely sources for new buckles. Thrift stores, flea markets, garage sales, and specialty shows (such as military or cowboy antique and collectible shows) are also sure to have some used buckles to get you started.

Prices can range from a few dollars up to several hundred depending upon age, condition, and the material that the buckle is crafted from. If you like old buckles, buy a good price guide and become familiar with the styles and values of those listed. Talk with other collectors, dealers, and even museum curators who are familiar with early buckles. Once your collection begins to grow, there are several options for displaying them.

Naturally, belt buckles can be worn so others can see them; however, when you have more than just a handful, you will probably need other display options. Display cases, flat boards covered with a neutral fabric, or simply lining a shelf with the buckles can make very attractive exhibits.

Collecting buckles is a great way to preserve history, celebrate pop culture, experiment with fashion, and express your interests. The best reason to collect belt buckles, though, is because it's fun!

Related Collectibles: belts and ladies belt pins from the 1800s

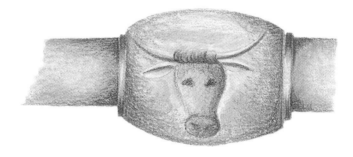

Birthday Collectibles

"The birthday of my life
Is come, my love is come to me."
Christina Georgina Rossetti, 1830-1894

Birthdays are often remembered as some of the happiest days of our lives, and with the prospect of presents and friends dressed in their Sunday best, we usually want the day to go on forever. It's no wonder, then, that many people enjoy collecting things that are related to this special celebration!

Birthday collectibles include party favors, hats, candles, noisemakers, streamers, revolving cake stands, plates, and other decorations. Cards, invitations, and printed table cloths are also nice additions to a birthday collection, and today, the selection of birthday collectibles is almost endless.

Many grocery, discount, card, gift, and specialty stores offer an array of birthday items. If you want to see a really impressive assortment of birthday goodies, then go to a party store. These stores specialize in party accessories of all kinds and include many hard-to-find birthday decorations. New birthday collectibles range in price from under $1 to over $20. If you want something with a little more history, then consider looking at secondhand sales.

Shop garage sales, flea markets, antique stores, and church bazaars to find used or antique birthday collectibles. While it can be a little more challenging to find birthday collectibles this way, it can also be quite rewarding. Recent finds at second-hand sales include a Kermit the Frog birthday table-cloth, a Mickey Mouse cake plate, and a revolving birth-day cake stand from the 1960s. While these items may not be valuable, they are probably difficult to find. The good news is that each of these birthday collectibles were priced at less that $5.

Collect birthday items throughout the year, or save decorations from your own birthday celebration. For an even more personal approach, collect only the things that pertain to your birth date or year.

Magazines, newspapers, sheet music, or just about anything that was published on your birth date or during your birth year can make an interesting collection. Read about current events, trends, prices, and how the world was viewed at the time of your birth. A little research at the local library, and some selective photocopying, can help you customize a collection of clips for a birthday scrapbook.

You might even want to look back in history and record some of the more notable events. Who else shares your same birth date? What inventions were announced? What milestones were achieved? By using your birth date or year as a starting point, you can develop an interesting collection of birthday history.

Other birthday collectibles—such as calendars and calendar plates—are wonderful reminders of your first days on earth, and they are easily displayed on the wall or on a shelf.

Regardless of which direction your collection takes you, happy birthday and happy collecting!

Related Collectibles: holiday collectibles

35

Books

....

"The love of learning, the sequestered nooks,
And all the sweet serenity of books."
Henry Wadsworth Longfellow, 1807-1882

The ancient Mesopotamians wrote on clay tablets, early Egyptians penned their thoughts on papyrus scrolls—some that measured 30 feet or more—and in 1445, Johann Gutenberg invented the printing press. Over the past 500 years, book production has come a long way, leaving a great and diverse collectible in its wake.

Books are passports to any place, any time, any culture. Sail the seven seas, blast into space, climb the tallest mountain, or learn about the formation of the earth. You can experience all of this, and more, between the front and back covers of a book. It's no wonder, then, that books are treasured by many collectors—young and old alike. With so many books and so many subjects, the only question is: What type of books do you want to collect?

Some collectors specialize in rare first editions, spending a small fortune on a single book. Fortunately, for the aspiring book collector, this isn't the only option. Fine book collections can focus on a single topic such as birds, include a broad category of writing such as science fiction, or feature the complete works of a specific author, such as William Shakespeare. Other types of books to consider are signed copies, pop-up, coffee table, paperbacks, or contemporary first editions.

Sometimes it can be tricky for even an experienced book dealer to tell if a book is a first edition. If there isn't a date on the front of the title page, but there is a date on the *back* of the title page, you may have a first edition. It's often easier to rule out a first edition than to say with certainty that it is a first edition. Look at the printing history and the copyright date. The printing history lists the dates of each edition. The copyright notice tells who owns the rights to the book. If these dates do not match, the book is probably not a first edition. If you collect first editions, it is wise to befriend a knowledgeable book dealer who can help determine the printing history of any books you are unsure of; however, as long as your books cost only a few dollars, you needn't be too concerned about making mistakes. Another thing to keep in mind as you look for books is condition.

Books were not made to withstand rough treatment or even the normal wear and tear of decades of use. Although it is difficult to find used books in perfect condition, there are some guidelines to follow. The books in your collection should be complete, free of scribbles, dirt, or other marks, and they should not have any major damage such as tears or loose pages. Also, whenever possible, hardcover books should be wrapped in their original dust jackets.

If you decide, however, to collect books from a certain series, condition can sometimes be a secondary concern. Just finding all the books in a particular series may be a major accomplishment. For that reason, you should probably buy each volume that you see, regardless of its condition. Over time, if you find another copy of a book in the series that's in better condition than yours, you can buy it to improve the quality of your collection. The key to assembling a complete series in good condition is to buy what you see and keep looking.

New books are sold almost everywhere. Grocery, discount, department, gift, and specialty stores all carry books of some kind. Today's "super" book stores, which are huge, are great places for the bibliophile or book lover to pick up new books, too, but buying retail isn't the only way to build a collection.

Used, rare, or out-of-print books can be purchased from a variety of secondhand outlets. Church bazaars, garage sales, "Friends of the Library" book sales, and flea markets offer a variety of inexpensive used books. Occasionally, household auctions and estate sales include an interesting assortment of books. Also, there is no better way to spend a rainy afternoon than browsing through a secondhand bookstore. As you start bringing books home, make sure to keep them in a safe place.

If possible, keep all of your books on shelves in a room that isn't too humid. Mold grows in moist environments and it can ruin books. To keep the covers and spines from fading, select shelving that is away from direct sun light. Also, frequently dust your books and look for signs of insect damage. If you notice discoloration or holes, talk with a friendly book dealer to see what can be done.

Books are one of the best collectibles available, and they can get you started on a lifelong adventure of knowledge, intrigue, and fun!

Related Collectibles: bookmarks, bookplates, and bookends

Bottles

....

"Shake and shake
The catsup bottle.
None will come,
And then a lot'll."

Richard Armour, 1906-1989

From baby to catsup bottles, milk to bitters bottles, and perfume to poison bottles, the life cycle of man can be traced. Although there may be 50 or more different bottles in your home, storing everything from soda pop to dish soap, these modern containers have ancient beginnings.

Hollow gourds or animal skins probably served as the first "bottles." Water, oil, perfume, and other liquids were transported in these early flasks. Later, the ancient Egyptians coiled threads of molten glass around clay or earthen molds to create some of the earliest glass bottles. As far back as the first century B.C., Roman glass blowers formed bottles by blowing air through a tube to shape the molten glass. Blown-glass bottles were the preferred vessels for ancient man's pills and potions, and the demand for them continually increased.

American businesses showed a preference toward glass for packaging their products beginning in the late eighteenth century. By the nineteenth century, the mass production of bottles was widespread. Bottles of all shapes, sizes, and colors held ink, medicine, milk, soda, spirits, vinegar, and other liquids. The number and variety of glass bottles used in packaging has left a huge legacy for today's bottle collectors, and depending upon whether you collect old or new bottles, you might find that bottles multiply even more quickly than rabbits!

As you might suspect, antique bottles are generally more difficult to find and are more costly than the new bottles, therefore, it's probably wise to look for bottles made in 1940 and later. During this time frame there was a great variety of perfume, milk, and soda bottles manufactured. Perhaps the best known perfume bottles come from the company that makes Avon products. Avon bottles are shaped like dolls, cars, and animals, and although some of these figural bottles are rare and quite costly, many can be found at flea markets, church bazaars, and garage sales for just a few dollars. While some collectors look for any and all Avon bottles, others specialize in a particular shape, such as cars or animals, but if the sweet smell of perfume, cologne, or toilet water doesn't have you sniffing around for bottles, then how about milk?

The 1970s saw the disappearance of home-delivered milk in the United States. Everything from sweet cream in half-pint servings to one-gallon reservoirs of fresh milk were delivered in glass bottles bearing the name and logo of the dairy. Today, these bottles turn up at garage sales, flea markets, antique stores, and secondhand shops with great frequency. With prices ranging from a dollar and up, milk bottles can make a fine collection. The dairy's name and logo are often painted on the bottles, but some have raised or embossed images. The bottles with raised lettering or pictures are the most desirable and often the most expensive.

To add a little fizz to your collecting, consider soda pop bottles. Soda bottles are great to collect! Without spending a fortune, a soda bottle collection can include examples from local, regional, or international bottlers. Old soda bottles which once carried the product of unknown companies, can often be found at antique stores and flea markets for just a few dollars. Because of the soaring popularity of Coca-Cola, Dr. Pepper, and other major brands, however, it's often difficult to find early examples of bottles from these companies which are affordable—but don't lose heart—there are many other bottles to collect.

Ink, bitters, medicine, bleach, oil, and syrup bottles are prized by many collectors, and if you know where to look, you'll discover other unique bottles to add to your collection. Old bottles can be found in a variety of places. Antique stores, auctions, flea markets, and church bazaars are wonderful hunting grounds for bottles of all kinds. And, if you like beating the bushes, antique bottles can sometimes be found at sites where old homes or towns used to sit.

Once you begin, give some thought to how you will display your collection. Bottles are usually displayed on shelves or tables where they can be admired, and while some collectors display them empty, others fill them with beads, buttons, or marbles to give them a splash of color. Milk bottle collectors often display their bottles filled with small, white, Styrofoam balls. This makes it easier to read the name of the dairy, and the white balls in the bottle resemble milk.

So, if you like bottles, don't put a cork in your enthusiasm—go out and start collecting!

Related Collectibles: bottle caps, bottle openers, and cans

BOXES

....

*"I would like a simple life
Yet all night I am laying
poems away in a long box."*
Anne Sexton, 1928-1974

It's a safe and special place. It's where we put treasures, lock away secrets, and store belongings. It's round, square, oval, oblong, or shaped like any one of a hundred common things. An egg, a gingerbread man, a house, a lute, and a butterfly have all inspired craftsmen to create boxes in their images. Boxes of every size, shape, and color have been used by mankind throughout history.

The Pharaohs of ancient Egypt had jeweled boxes filled with the riches of their kingdoms; Japanese Washi boxes preserved decorated scrolls in places of honor; and sophisticates in eighteenth-century Europe carried snuff and patches (beauty spots) in delicate enamel boxes. The function of boxes has remained constant throughout history: to contain, preserve or honor items of special importance. Over time, however, the material and design of boxes has varied greatly.

Boxes forged of precious metals, crafted in papier-mâché or oriental lacquer, tooled in copper, and carved from wood are but a few examples of the variety. It is the diversity and utility of boxes which has inspired collectors to seek these containers out as a genuine collectible.

Among the most popular are cigar and hat boxes. These boxes are often decorated with lithographs of country scenes, city scapes, animals, and people. The quality of the artwork and the number of subjects, make these boxes especially attractive to collectors. Boxes from the Victorian era through the 1920s frequently have scenes depicting their era. Women in long flowing skirts, men sporting handlebar mustaches, and early automobiles are among the most popular subjects; however, many of the older versions of these boxes can be quite expensive—so you might want to look for modern boxes to get you started.

Tin boxes, particularly those that once contained fruit cakes, cookies, and candy make attractive additions to any box collection. Decorated with cowboys, teddy bears, and other designs that appeal to children, tin boxes are plentiful and varied enough to keep a young collector interested for quite a while, and holiday tins, with pictures of Santa Claus, the Easter Bunny, or other seasonal designs are the focus of entire collections. If tin boxes aren't of much interest to you, however, there are other ways to build an interesting box collection.

Collecting single purpose boxes (such as jewelry or pencil boxes) product containers (such as tea or cigar boxes) or boxes made of your favorite material can be a great way to begin a box collection. All you have to know is where to find them.

Gift, discount, department, and other retail stores offer a variety of products in boxes that can get a collection off to a good start. In fact, many of these stores sell empty boxes that can go right into a collection. For old or antique boxes, visit flea markets, antique shops, garage sales, church bazaars, and other secondhand sales. It's fairly simple to find boxes, and displaying them isn't any more difficult.

Set, stack, or line boxes up on shelves, tables, or in cupboards. To make a box collection more interesting, you might display them in the rooms that make the most sense. For example, cereal boxes look great in the kitchen, hat boxes display well in bedrooms, and pencil boxes are quite natural in studies or offices.

As with any other collectible, the most important thing is to collect what you like. Boxes are a fun and practical collectible. If you ever run out of space to keep your box collection, you can store one inside the other!

Related Collectibles: box labels, advertising, and bottles or other containers

16

Building Blocks and Construction Toys

....

"All by myself, wrapped in my thoughts,
And building castles in Spain and in France."
Charles d' Orleans, 1394-1465

Build a castle fortress, construct an expansive bridge, or design an entire city using only your imagination and a collection of building blocks or construction toys. For many generations, young architects have laid a foundation of fun using wooden blocks, Lincoln Logs, Erector Sets, Legos, Tinker Toys, and other construction toys. A love of building and an appreciation for design are the cornerstones of a construction toy collection.

Since at least the Victorian era, sets of building blocks with lithographed pictures pasted to the wooden cubes have kept many young builders busy on rainy days. Piling block upon block, great towers and mysterious structures were created only to be knocked down by a younger brother or sister. Carved wooden blocks lettered with the ABCs, teaching toddlers that "A is for apple," have long been a favorite with collectors. Also, using lettered blocks to spell out names or holiday messages such as "Merry Christmas" has been a decorator's trick for many years.

Building blocks, especially the early ones, make a great addition to other collections as well. The display of a doll collection can often be enhanced by placing stacks of square blocks around a few of the dolls. Likewise, a collection of toy cars, stuffed toys, or tops can quite naturally be displayed with a few well-positioned blocks. Use blocks to build a more interesting display or look to other construction toys to build something even bigger.

Over 80 years ago, the first Lincoln Logs were placed in the hands of young toy pioneers. Building forts, cabins, towers, and anything that the tiny logs and the imagination could produce, meant hours of pure construction fun. Lincoln Logs have changed little since they were first introduced and can be bought at toy and department stores. The major difference is the addition of plastic parts in the new sets. Older sets from the 1960s, or earlier, came with wooden chimneys and green roof slats. Even the designs of the boxes which contained the early logs are very collectible. With old or new Lincoln Logs, collectors are bound to have a great time building cabins, forts, and Old West settlements.

If you're a collector with a more modern approach to construction, though, consider collecting Erector Sets. Beginning in the early 1900s, the A.C. Gilbert Company produced many different Erector Sets. With metal girders, angles, plates, nuts, bolts, gears, and, in some cases, electric motors, these sets gave young engineers everything they needed to build realistic miniatures. The early Erector Sets were sold either as complete projects, or in general boxed sets. Complete instructions and all of the parts needed to build a steam engine, an action helicopter, a truck, a rocket launcher, or an amusement park were packed in the project Erector Sets. These special sets are among the most popular with collectors of building and construction toys; however, they also tend to be very expensive. For more affordable sets, take a walk through the isles of your favorite toy store to find a variety of new sets.

On the other hand, if brightly colored, interlocking bricks build your enthusiasm, then how about Lego or other compatible blocks? Many different Lego sets with instructions on how to build an airplane, a car, a rocket, and other interesting structures can be purchased for a few dollars. Larger Lego and Lego-compatible sets with hundreds of pieces can provide a lifetime of unbridled creativity. Build an airplane with a propeller that spins, a grand tower that stands as tall as a tree, or a castle with a working drawbridge. The only limits will be the height of your ceiling and the number of bricks you have—and if all of these building and construction toys don't keep you busy, then look for others.

Tinker Toys, Tower-ifics, and other connectable, stackable, linkable building toys provide so many options that it boggles the mind. All you have to do is look, just a little bit, to find a wide variety of toys to choose from.

Toy stores are the most obvious place to look for construction and building toys, but not the only place. Specialty, nature, and gift stores often feature unique building toys that sometimes defy description, and although garage sales, church bazaars, and other secondhand sales may not be the best bet, building blocks and other construction toys are occasionally offered in good condition, and at reasonable prices.

Once you have a few construction toy sets, it's time to think about how you'll display them. Perhaps the best way to show off your collection is to build something. Admirers will not only appreciate the toys themselves, but also your handy-work as an engineer.

Whether you specialize in a single type of building block or construction set, or assemble a variety of sets, you are sure to build a great collection.

Related Collectibles: models and puzzles

Business Cards

*"It is with literature as with law or empire –
an established name is an estate in tenure,
or a throne in possession."*

Edgar Allan Poe, 1809-1848

As a social grace, visitors in the Victorian era announced their arrival by presenting the housemaid or butler with a calling card. This card, simple yet elegant in design, gave the name of the caller. Visitors conveyed the reason for calling, by turning down one corner of the card or another. Depending upon how the card was folded, the purpose could be to express heart-felt condolences, to say good-bye, or just to say "Hello." While the practice of presenting a calling card for personal visits has long since been forgotten, companies often provide their employees with business cards. It is common for a business person to present a card with their name, title, company name, address, and telephone number on it to anyone who might be interested in the company's products or services.

At some point in time, an enterprising collector decided that business cards would make a great collectible. Today, collectors of all ages add business cards to their collections each day. In an effort to build the largest, most diverse, and unique business card collection, collectors ask friends, relatives, acquaintances, and even strangers to contribute a card to their collection. It is such a small request that most of the people asked gladly give their card. Collecting business cards is a very inexpensive hobby that can help you meet people and learn many interesting things.

Collecting business cards can be a fun way to find out about different jobs. Ask your parents, grandparents, and adult friends to help you collect cards from where they work. Then, based upon the title given on the card, find out what that person does at his or her job. A vexilliogist, for example, is someone who studies flags. A product manager, is someone who manages the technical design or marketing program for a specific product. An entomologist, is a scientist that studies insects. A nurse is someone who takes care of patients. There are many fascinating jobs that you can learn about while assembling your business card collection—and if you work hard and have a bit of luck, you can even learn about jobs in other states.

Perhaps the company that your parents, grandparents, or their friends work for has an office or a "sister" company in another state. If so, it might be easy for them to gather business cards from other states; however, you don't have to limit your collection only to our country's borders.

People in many different countries carry business cards. Wouldn't it be exciting to add a business card from Germany, Mexico, or Japan to your collection? Again, someone you know might have a business connection to someone in another country. If you are able to collect cards from several different countries, you might even specialize in foreign business cards. If neither you nor anyone you know has any connections to businesses in other states or countries, don't give up. It'll take a little bit of work, but you can write letters asking for cards for your collection.

Perhaps the easiest place to begin your search for out-of-state or foreign business cards is in your own home. Look on the products sitting on the shelves in the pantry, or the furniture that fills each room, or on your home appliances. Chances are, there is a customer service address or telephone number either on the product itself or on the warranty. With your parents' permission, write a letter to the companies that manufactured the products in your home. The letter should say that your household buys the company's products, that you are putting together an interstate or international business card collection, and that you would like to have a business card from someone in their company. Since most companies respond to customer letters, the chances are very good that you'll get a business card in the mail. This same approach may work if you specialize in certain types of jobs.

If, for example, you decide to collect business cards from politicians, try writing selected politicians a letter to explain who you are and what you want. It is likely that you will get a positive response to your requests—especially if it's an election year.

Collecting business cards is a fun, educational, and affordable hobby. Display options for your cards include arranging them in inexpensive store-bought frames, placing them in photograph albums, storing them in cardboard boxes, or filing them alphabetically in a business card holder which can be bought at an office supply store.

The most important things to remember when collecting business cards are to be polite when requesting cards, to have fun, and get to the business of collecting!

Related Collectibles: printed business stationery, business embossed or rubber stamps, or business card holders

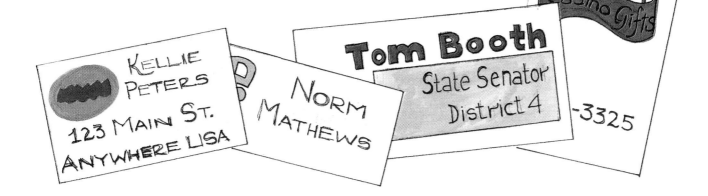

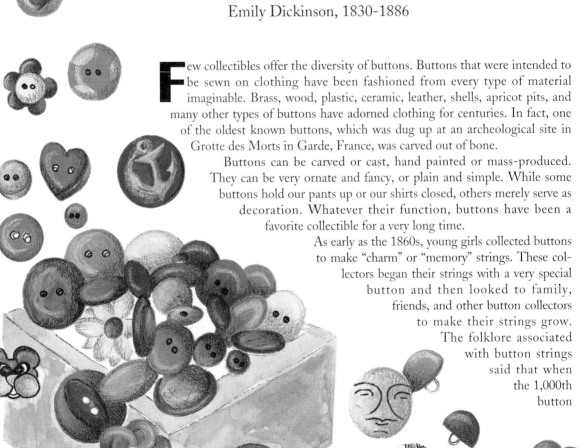

18

BUTTONS

....

"Brazil? He twirled a Button –
Without a glance my way –
'But – Madam – is there nothing else –
That We can show – Today?'"

Emily Dickinson, 1830-1886

Few collectibles offer the diversity of buttons. Buttons that were intended to be sewn on clothing have been fashioned from every type of material imaginable. Brass, wood, plastic, ceramic, leather, shells, apricot pits, and many other types of buttons have adorned clothing for centuries. In fact, one of the oldest known buttons, which was dug up at an archeological site in Grotte des Morts in Garde, France, was carved out of bone.

Buttons can be carved or cast, hand painted or mass-produced. They can be very ornate and fancy, or plain and simple. While some buttons hold our pants up or our shirts closed, others merely serve as decoration. Whatever their function, buttons have been a favorite collectible for a very long time.

As early as the 1860s, young girls collected buttons to make "charm" or "memory" strings. These collectors began their strings with a very special button and then looked to family, friends, and other button collectors to make their strings grow. The folklore associated with button strings said that when the 1,000th button was added, the young girl's true love would appear. Although many young ladies failed to string 1,000 buttons, they still enjoyed collecting—and some even found their sweethearts!

Early collections often began with the leftover buttons from sewing projects. Later, buttons off of old clothing (or trading buttons with others) kept the collections going. Collectors used to store their buttons in special boxes, sew them on a velvet cloth to display them, or string them on long pieces of twine.

Today, button collecting offers an affordable, virtually unlimited collecting experience. To get a better idea of the variety of buttons available, just look in your own home. You may even find the beginnings of a collection in your closet!

The best place to find interesting buttons is on used clothing. Clothes with buttons suitable for collecting can be found at garage sales, and church bazaars. Also, mason jars, cigar boxes, and bags of buttons are frequently sold at antique stores and flea markets. Additionally, buttons are often available at antiques and collectibles shows. Prices range from a few cents for an individual button, to hundreds of dollars for rare, complete button sets.

To narrow down your search, you might want to specialize. Some collectors look for old buttons made of glass, while others prefer hand-painted buttons. Many collectors look for buttons off of old uniforms. The shiny brass buttons from police, firemen, and fraternal order uniforms are wonderful collectibles. Keep in mind, however, that if you specialize in a specific type of button, it might take more time and money to build up a strong collection.

Regardless of what type of buttons you collect, though, displaying them can be half the fun! Historically, buttons have either been displayed on a long string or sewn on to a framed cloth; however, there are many ways to show off your buttons. Sew them on to cardboard sheets and put them in a three-ring binder, place flat buttons in a photograph album, sew them on clothing, make a button necklace, or fill glass jars, vases, or bottles with the colorful disks. Use your imagination and try a variety of display options.

With so many different types of buttons to choose from, collecting them can be a lot of fun!

Related Collectibles: button hooks, pins, brooches

CAMERA Collectibles

··

"I am a camera with its shutter open, quite passive, recording, not thinking. Recording the man shaving at the window opposite and the woman in the kimono washing her hair. Some day, all this will have to be developed, carefully printed, fixed."

Christopher William Bradshaw Isherwood, 1904-1986

The human eye, it is said, is the oldest camera known to man. Using light, the eye captures an image and transmits a picture to the brain, letting us see the things around us. With all of the beauty and wonder in the world, it only makes sense that man would design a machine that would allow us to keep what we see, long after it's gone. The machine is, of course, the camera. From this invention came a collectible that's rapidly being snapped up by collectors.

The camera is nearly 150 years old. In the early days of photography, only a handful of people knew how to take pictures. Being a photographer not only meant taking the picture, but also carefully mixing chemicals in order to produce a picture. In the beginning, photography was much more of a science for chemists, than an art for the masses. In fact, it was not unusual for even the most experienced photographer to struggle to produce a single good picture.

Then, in 1888, George Eastman invented a camera that made it easy for almost anyone to take good pictures. The original Kodak camera came loaded with enough chemically treated film to snap off 100 pictures. When the pictures had been taken, the camera was mailed back to Eastman's company for developing. Eastman's motto was "You press the button, we do the rest." True to his word, Eastman's Kodak revolutionized photography. Ever since then, hundreds of cameras and related equipment have been developed to make taking pictures even easier—and with every innovation, the list of camera collectibles grows larger.

As new cameras are introduced, older models are tucked in closets, stashed on shelves, and forgotten. This is great news for camera collectors.

For just a few dollars, early cameras and equipment can be picked up by alert collectors. Old cameras can be found at garage sales, flea markets, and church bazaars—most at very reasonable prices. Simple folding, box, pocket, and other manual cameras are pretty easy to find, and tripods, slide projectors, and movie projectors frequently turn up at bargain prices.

Other unique cameras, such as stereo, miniature, or those with accessory lenses, may be expensive and difficult to find; however, if you see one of these highly collectible cameras at a price that you can afford, snap it up! Every once in a while, there will be a great bargain waiting for the patient and persistent collector.

There are many ways to display such a collection. Certainly, cameras and other equipment display well on shelves, tables, or in cupboards, but there are other options, as well. Try positioning a few old cameras on free-standing tripods, or hang cameras by the strap from either the ceiling or on the wall. While this isn't a typical approach, it will make your exhibit more interesting. To enhance your display, you can use photographs you took as the background.

Collecting cameras is a good way to trace the development of photography and, hopefully, supply you with some usable equipment. Just load the film, snap away, and smile—you're a camera collector!

Related Collectibles: photography and camera advertising and packaging

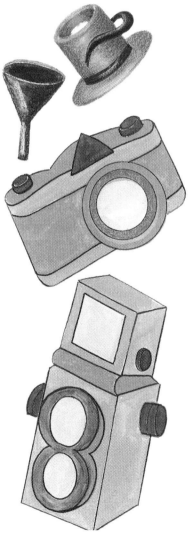

20

Candles

....

"My candle burns at both ends,
It will not last the night;
But, ah, my Foes, and, oh, my Friends—
It gives a lovely light."

Edna St. Vincent Millay, 1892-1950

The light from millions of candles have illuminated the path of man for thousands of years. Candles have set the stage for ceremonies, holidays, and celebrations. Though the function of candles has remained the same, their form has changed from simple useful designs, to complex, artistic sculptures.

The earliest candles were made by dipping fiber wicks into a hot vat of beeswax or tarrow (animal fat). These handmade candles were expensive and burned only by the very wealthy, or on special occasions. It wasn't until 1834, when a candle molding machine was invented, that the mass production of candles was possible. Molded candles were much more affordable than hand-dipped ones, and use of candle light spread quickly. Today, the variety of shapes, colors, and sizes makes candles appealing to many collectors.

A stroll down the isles of even the smallest department store should take you to candle country. In housewares, long tapered candles used for adding "atmosphere" to quiet, intimate meals, come in a variety of colors. Near the greeting cards, short pin-striped or number-shaped birthday candles wait for an invitation to a party. In the "seasonal" isle, look for ghost or bat Halloween candles, turkey or horn-of-plenty-shaped Thanksgiving candles, or Santa or snowmen candles for the happiest of holidays—and this is only the tip of the candlewick.

Flowers, football players, dogs, cars, ice cream sundaes, snow men, trains, and many other figural candles await the candle collector. Designer candles including hand-dipped beeswax, multi-colored sculpted, and sand candles add a dash of elegance to any collection, and the variety of shapes, colors, and sizes is almost unlimited.

Many candles are adorned with glitter, synthetic flowers, sequins, or other decorations. Any of these candles can, by themselves, make up an entire collection. Additionally, jasmine, cinnamon, strawberry, and other fragrances are often added to candle wax to sweeten their appeal. The elegance, diversity, and abundance of candles truly does make it a great collecting category.

Unlike most of the collectibles in this book, collectors can rarely find good candles at garage sales or flea markets. Secondhand candles are often burned, broken, or covered with grime. For this reason, look in gift shops, department stores, candle shops, and party stores to find candles for your collection. Additionally, craft shows, factory outlets, party stores, mail order catalogues, and historical fairs are good sources.

The price of candles range from a dollar or less, to over one hundred, depending upon the complexity of the design, size, and the type of wax that was used. Beeswax, hand-dipped, and carved candles are often the most expensive.

Once you begin collecting them, you will want to display them. Candles can be displayed in seasonal arrangements, lined up on shelves or used throughout the house to accent the furnishings. Just choose the places to display your candles carefully.

To protect your investment, keep in mind that candles require special care. First, make sure that you never light a candle without adult supervision. Many accidental fires are started by an unattended candle flame. Second, candles should be stored at moderate to cool temperatures. Extreme heat warps and melts them. If you can, place your candles in a closed cabinet or glass case to protect them from dust.

Finally, be prepared to talk about your unique collection. After all, candles can really light up a conversation!

Related Collectibles: candlesticks, candle molds, candle snuffers

Candy Containers

....

"Sweets to the sweet: Farewell!"
William Shakespeare, 1564-1616

The American candy industry saw phenomenal growth beginning in the mid-1800s with the mass-production of hand-held treats. By 1900, there were about 1,000 American candy companies, and by 1920, there were over 3,000 manufacturers turning out a variety of confections. Sugar candies such as jelly beans, butter creams, rock candy, licorice, and a variety of chocolates tempted the most discriminating tastes, and, as if the candy wasn't tempting enough, many manufacturers packaged their treats in charming containers. Papier-mâché bunnies, highly decorated tins, and figural glass containers became as popular as their candy. While some, of these early candy containers can be quite rare and expensive, many new, less expensive candy containers are introduced each year.

The number of plastic candy containers alone is enough to keep even the most avid collector hopping faster than the Easter Bunny. Just take a walk down the candy isle at your favorite grocery, department, or convenience store. Plastic candy containers shaped like teeth, sharks, Band-Aid boxes, cars, and more line the shelves. Plastic candy dispensers with famous cartoon characters, celebrities, monsters, and other shapes are plentiful as well. Look for noise-making, candy-filled containers like portable telephones with beeping buttons. This is candy container collecting for the twenty-first century at its best—and the collecting options are even sweeter if you specialize in holiday containers.

Plastic hearts, Easter bunnies, Santas, and cane-shaped containers filled with delicious chocolates, hard candies, or creams make welcome additions to any collection, and many holiday tins give seasonal collectors something to celebrate. A sharp eye and a few ready dollars can help your candy container collection get off to a sweet start.

The best place to look for modern candy containers is in your local drug or discount store. The prices for candy is generally lower in these stores than in convenience or grocery stores. The prices for plastic containers should range from fifty cents to a few dollars depending upon the type of container and candy. Filled tins can cost up to fifty or more dollars if filled with fine imported chocolates. While one benefit to collecting brand new candy containers is that there is a treat in every one, you might also look for secondhand containers. This will allow you to add candy containers that are no longer being used to package candy.

Recent candy containers are showing up more frequently at flea markets and garage sales. While the tins are seen more frequently, plastic ones are also beginning to appear. When these modern containers are offered for sale on the secondhand market, it's usually for one of two reasons: Either the seller has just cleaned out the cupboards—or the seller is guessing that the price of the container will go up, and has, therefore, asked a premium price for it. Be careful when you buy used candy containers. If the price isn't fifty cents or less, you might want to do some homework to find out if the container is still available at the corner store. When in doubt about the value of a container, don't buy it.

As your candy container collection grows, think about whether you want to invest in some of the older containers. Figural glass, papier-mâché, tin, and composition containers are wonderful collectibles. Be careful, though. Many of these have been reproduced, and they almost always carry an expensive price tag. Before adding antique containers to your collection, buy a good price guide and become familiar with the styles and values. Also, if you find dealers who specialize in old candy containers, learn as much as you can from them. Ask about the history, manufacturers, designs, values, collector's clubs, and display tips.

Most candy container collections are displayed on shelves or in china cupboards. Holiday containers, cars, animals, and other categories are often arranged by subject. Use other decorative items such as posters, toys, and advertising pieces to create a unique and personal display. The only limit to creating creative candy container displays is your imagination.

Collecting candy containers is fun, and it can be a very sweet experience!

Related Collectibles: candy molds, candy machines, gumball machines

22

CANNING JARS

....

"Come fill up my cup, come fill up my can,
Come saddle your horses, and call up you men;
Come open the West Port, and let me gang free,
And it's room for the bonnets of Bonny Dundee!"
Sir Walter Scott, 1771-1832

Today, many people scour flea markets, garage sales, antique stores, and church bazaars in search of canning jars. They remind us of home cooking, gardening, and grandma's preserves; however, even though they tend to remind us of a simpler time, their invention stemmed from a complex problem.

Canning jars were born as a result of a contest. In 1795, the French government offered a prize to anyone who could keep food fresh for the troops in the field. In 1810, a French chef named Nicolas, was awarded the prize. Nicolas discovered that when food is heated and packaged in an air-tight container, it remains edible for a very long time. Out of Nicolas' efforts, the canning jar was born. Today, the canning jar is not only a favorite with home canners, but also with collectors.

Canning jars, which are also called "Fruit jars," have been manufactured by many different companies. The early jars were handmade by skilled craftsmen. You can tell if a jar was handmade by feeling the rim. If the rim is pitted and feels rough to the touch, it was probably handmade. If the rim is smooth with a rounded rim, the jar was probably more recently machine-made. Once you determine if the jar was hand- or machine-made, look for other clues to its past.

Embossed trademarks might help identify the maker and determine when it was made. Although many jars bear patent dates from the 1800s, it does not necessarily mean that they were made that long ago. To track down the manufacturer and the age of any given jar, you have to be part historian and part detective. Check your local library or bookstore to see if they have a book on canning jars. There are a few books that identify canning jar trademarks and provide information on the manufacturers.

For example, several different Canadian companies used crowns as their trademark. Each crown looks slightly different and depending upon the size of the crown, the shape, and how it was decorated, a knowledgeable collector may be able to identify the manufacturer. A heart-shaped crown with dots over each hump, with a stick man on each side of the crown, indicates that Burlington Glass Works made the jar. It's important to remember, though, that a single manufacturer's trademark may vary over time or appear different on the various size jars.

Pints, quarts, and half gallon jars were made in the United States. Although Canadian companies manufactured these same sizes, they are shaped somewhat differently and may appear to be different sizes. The pint jars are probably the most popular but they are also the most difficult to find. Pint jars are easy to display, they look nice, and some collectors believe that over time, antique pint jars will become the most valuable.

Old canning jars can be found at antique shows, auctions, garage sales, flea markets, and at other secondhand sales. Probably the best way to begin your collection, though, is to ask friends and relatives if they have any jars they no longer use.

Look for canning jars in good condition, without cracks or nicks, and collect only the ones you like. In the end, if you like how canning jars look on the shelf, or if you used them as planters, drinking glasses, or to store marbles, then you'll not only have a fine collection, but you'll also be a happy collector!

Related Collectibles: canning lids, jelly jars, and bottles

CEREAL PREMIUMS

*"Mares eat oats,
and lambs eat oats,
and little kids eat ivy.
A kid'll eat ivy too,
wouldn't you?"*

Anonymous Nursery Rhyme

O f course you'll eat oats . . . and corn, wheat, rice, and other grains that breakfast cereal is made of. What could be better than a big bowl of your favorite cereal on a sunny Saturday morning? I'll tell you what. A big bowl of your favorite cereal and the free toy inside the box. For many years, the prize inside, and the toy that can be sent away for, have called out to children passing through the cereal isle. "I want that one, Mommy," the toddler cries. Not because sugar-coated puffed spinach pops is the little tike's favorite, but because in specially marked boxes you will find a super-fast, dyno-car with "real" exhaust. Even though free toys rule in the cereal isle today, it wasn't always that way.

In the 1860s, at a hospital in Battle Creek, Michigan, sheets of baked dough were ground up in an effort to develop healthful additions to the vegetarian diet. C.W. Post, who was a patient at the hospital, and W.C. Kellogg, improved upon this method, and America's preferred breakfast food—cereal—was born. In the beginning, cereal was an adult food, but over time, it would find its way into children's bowls.

In 1949, Sam Gold, a Chicago salesman began visiting cereal manufacturers to see if they would offer his toys as premiums. It took very little convincing, since radio premiums had proven so successful. In no time, box top toys and other kid-appealing freebies graced the cereal boxes lining the shelves. Sam Gold's legacy is an ideal collectible for anyone willing to munch, crunch, and either dig or send away for the prize.

Everything from stickers to toy cars, dolls, and games can be had for the price of one or more boxes of a certain brand of cereal. Larger items such as videos, T-shirts, and multi-piece toy sets are sometimes available for some proof-of-purchase seals plus a few dollars. Many of the offers include exclusive items that were made just for that cereal promotion. These "limited" editions are especially appealing to collectors wanting to assemble a unique sample of premiums, and there are certainly a lot of cereal companies giving you the opportunity to build your collection by eating their brand. The next time you stroll down the cereal isle at your local supermarket, just read the front of the boxes.

Trading cards, stickers, and mini-posters featuring the faces of athletes, movie stars, television personalities, and cartoon characters are popular give-a-ways. These are sometimes printed right on the back of the box or included inside. That's what makes these cereal premiums so appealing to collectors. There's no need to eat six boxes of a particular brand, to send away for, or to pay anything extra to get them. Just buy one of the "specially marked boxes," and get one or more collectibles inside. Nothing could be easier, and many collectors build their collections on just what comes in the box. There are others, though, who are willing to go a bit further to add something special to their collections.

For two proof-of-purchase seals and $11.95, one cereal maker offers a commemorative mini-car collection. Another advertises a video for three proof-of-purchase seals and $3.95. Towels, remote control cars, backpacks, and many other items—most with the cereal logo prominently printed on the front—are frequently offered. The price of the item may not make it an especially "good deal," but collectors will find that it is worth the extra effort to add it to their collections.

While plucking premiums directly from the cereal companies might be a great way to build a collection, it isn't the only way. Premiums once seen in the cereal isle, are frequently sold at flea markets, garage sales, and church bazaars. These are great sources for collectors seeking to quickly build up or add a few "older" premiums to their collection. Be careful. Sometimes, the prices that are being asked are much higher than the premium's value. A good price guide and a trusted dealer can keep you from paying too much money for used premiums. Once you begin collecting, think of creative ways to display your breakfast-food finds.

Since it's possible to have T-shirts, posters, drinking glasses, toys, sports cards, and other seemingly mismatched items, you may face some unique display challenges. So, look in magazines, store windows, and in other people's homes for ideas. Also, use your own imagination to discover how to blend a diverse collection into an attractive exhibit.

For example, select one corner of your room to keep your collection in. Tack posters, T-shirts, and towels on the wall. Set drinking glasses, toys and baseball caps on shelves, and place sports cards and stickers in an open photo album on your dresser.

Collecting cereal premiums is fun and easy . . . especially if the cereal is already on the menu at your house. To borrow from a famous breakfast food spokesman . . . collect cereal premiums—"They're Great!"

Related Collectibles: cereal boxes, premiums from other products, toys from fast-food children's meals

Character Toys

"Six Characters in Search of an Author"
Title of a play by Luigi Pirandello, 1867-1936

At the heart of every character's identity is a writer or artist who brought that character to life. Whether fact or fiction, comic-strip or TV, a novel or the big screen, all characters have been created to appeal to folks like us. Everyone of us has our favorites. Cowboy stars, super heroes, cartoon characters, children's program hosts, monsters, and the familiar faces of television sitcoms, are among the most collectible character toys. There are thousands of characters for the young collector to choose from. Some are very rare and expensive, while others are common and can be purchased for just a few dollars. Perhaps the best place to begin looking for character toys is in the isles of a good toy or discount store.

Mickey Mouse, Winnie the Pooh, Bugs Bunny, Sylvester, the Smurfs, and other Saturday morning characters fill the stuffed toy isles. Action figures including Superman, Batman, The X-Men, Buzz Lightyear, Spiderman, and the popular Star Trek characters are flying off of the shelves at the speed of light. Barney, the Cat in the Hat, Big Bird, and other familiar characters appear in their own games, and dolls, vehicles, playsets, and lots of other toys feature today's popular characters.

The advantage to collecting new character toys is that they should be easy to find. The disadvantage is that retail prices are sometimes too expensive for young collectors. Before deciding to collect new character toys, talk with your parents to make sure that this collectible is within your budget. Keep in mind that the latest releases of any character toy is going to be more expensive than one that has been available for sometime. For example, when Disney's *Hunchback of Notre Dame* was first released, the toys sold for $3 and more. Within a year, the prices had dropped to as little as fifty cents.

Collecting is more fun when you can add several pieces each year to your collection. So, don't rule out looking for character toys at neighborhood sales, church bazaars, and flea markets. It's not unusual to find fairly new toys at a fraction of their retail costs at these secondhand sales.

Over the past few years, the prices of collectible character toys have gone up. Often, you will find "used" character toys at flea markets and antique stores priced well above their original retail values. In some cases, this makes sense due to the availability and demand for a specific character toy; however, some dealers are charging unfair prices. To keep from paying too much, get a good price guide and become familiar with current values. Remember, also, if a price seems too high, it's probably better not to buy the toy.

Character toys are highly sought after collectibles. Whether buying new or secondhand, there is a great variety to choose from. The only limits are the time and money it takes to buy them, and this is one collection that will build character as it grows!

Related Collectibles: other character collectibles such as cups, books, jewelry

25

Christmas Tree Ornaments

"Twas the night before Christmas, when all through the house
Not a creature was stirring, not even a mouse;
The stockings were hung by the chimney with care,
In hopes that St. Nicholas soon would be there;
The children were nestled all snug in their beds
While visions of sugar-plums danced in their heads . . . "

From *A Visit From St. Nicholas* by Clement C. Moore

1799-1863

In 300 AD, the good Bishop Nicholas showered needy children with love, kindness, and gifts. It was from the tales of his generosity that our own Santa Claus was born. During the eighteenth century, children saw Santa Claus as a gift giver to well-behaved youngsters, and a disciplinarian to the naughty. In Santa's early years it wasn't just his reputation that varied, he also looked different. Santa was often adorned in long flowing robes of yellow, blue, brown, green, and almost every color of the rainbow. It wasn't until an artist shared his version of Father Christmas that Santa became the jolly old elf that we know today.

Thomas Nast, an illustrator for *Harpers Weekly*, gets the credit for dressing Santa in his trademark red suit and for moving him to the North Pole. It's this image of Santa Claus that, for many people, symbolizes the true spirit of the holiday season.

Santa encourages us to celebrate, give to others, and enjoy what we are lucky enough to have. To some, Santa, the decorations, lights, and other trimmings are the stuff that collections are made of.

Perhaps the most popular Christmas collectibles are ornaments for the tree. Ornaments are beautiful, they don't take up much space, and they are practical if you decorate for the holiday. Also, if you buy ornaments at the right time, they're affordable.

The day after Christmas is the best time to build up your ornament collection. Super sales of up to 75% off of the retail prices of Christmas decorations lure many away from their pile of presents. Some collectors even line up before the stores open in order to get first crack at the holiday leftovers. Elegant angles; jolly round snowmen; festive animals; and other figural ornaments are waiting to be picked up at bargain prices. Ceramic, glass, wood, metal, and cloth ornaments offer even more variety. With so many kinds to choose from, some collectors narrow their focus.

Should you specialize in Christmas penguins, Santas, wreaths, candles, or tiny little buildings? Sure, almost any category will provide plenty of collecting and make a great display. How about collecting Disney, Hallmark, or Peanuts ornaments, or year, state, or name ornaments? Dogs, cars, snowmen, wreaths, bears, sleds, and other figures are yours for the collecting. In fact, there are hundreds of different types of ornaments to choose from, and that doesn't even include antique ornaments.

Elegant antique ornaments crafted in blown glass, crystal, or silver can be added as your collection matures. Antique tree ornaments can be found throughout the year at flea markets, garage sales, auctions, antique stores, and other secondhand sales. These are more difficult to find, and will cost considerably more than new ornaments, but it's an area of collecting you can grow into.

One very special way to add these fine old ornaments, is to ask grandparents, aunts, uncles, and other relatives to select one or two of their favorites from their own decorations for you. Just think how much more your collection will mean when it includes these family pieces.

If you're like most collectors, you'll want to see your ornaments year-round. Christmas tree ornaments can be displayed throughout the year on shelves, tables, or in cupboards. Try hanging them on a wall, cup rack, or make an ornament mobile. Try new arrangements to create a very personal, unique display.

The important thing is to enjoy your collection. If the song is correct, and Christmas is "the most wonderful day of the year," then you're sure to have a most wonderful time collecting Christmas tree ornaments!

Related Collectibles: other holiday collectibles

26

Circus Collectibles

"I like to go on picnics
and to outdoor movies, too;
It's fun to splash in swimming pools
and visit at the zoo.
But the best comes every summer
when my Daddy takes me down
To watch the folks parading
when the circus comes to town!"

From "When the Circus Comes to Town,"
a poem by Pansye H. Powell

Trick riding, juggling, tumbling, and wild animal acts can be traced back to antiquity, but it wasn't until 1768, when Philip Astley brought them all together in London, that they were performed in a ring. Astley's show marked the birth of the circus that we know today.

The 1890s were the Golden Age of the circus in the United States. Grand parades with trumpeting elephants, bareback riders, roaring lions and tigers, dancing dogs and monkeys, acrobats, and clowns transformed the sleepy streets of quiet towns into the stage for the "Greatest Show on Earth." The legacy of the circus, with its wealth of entertainers, has left behind circus collectibles for the young and young at heart.

Original circus programs and posters occasionally show up at antique stores, specialty shops, and antique and collectible shows. Often, these items are quite expensive, but don't lose heart. If you want to assemble a circus collection, there are many affordable pieces that can help you experience the magic of the "Big Top."

Books are, perhaps, some of the best circus collectibles. Through photographs, illustrations, and words, books can capture the heart and soul of the circus. Children's books such as Dr. Seuss' *If I ran the Circus* or biographies such as *P.T. Barnum, America's Greatest Showman*, highlight the personalities, performances, and the spirit of the circus. If you're interested in something a little closer to the real thing, and you're willing to do some research, you can start a circus scrapbook.

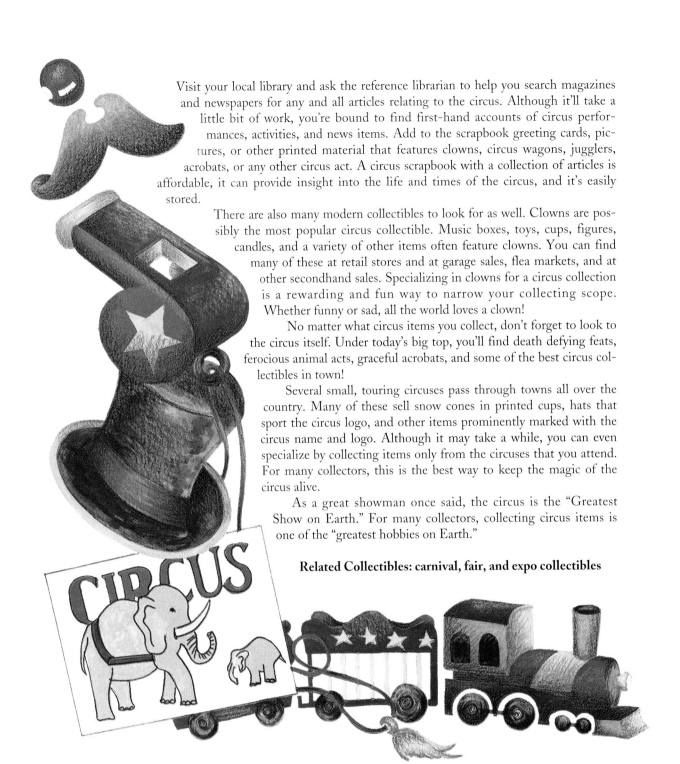

Visit your local library and ask the reference librarian to help you search magazines and newspapers for any and all articles relating to the circus. Although it'll take a little bit of work, you're bound to find first-hand accounts of circus performances, activities, and news items. Add to the scrapbook greeting cards, pictures, or other printed material that features clowns, circus wagons, jugglers, acrobats, or any other circus act. A circus scrapbook with a collection of articles is affordable, it can provide insight into the life and times of the circus, and it's easily stored.

There are also many modern collectibles to look for as well. Clowns are possibly the most popular circus collectible. Music boxes, toys, cups, figures, candles, and a variety of other items often feature clowns. You can find many of these at retail stores and at garage sales, flea markets, and at other secondhand sales. Specializing in clowns for a circus collection is a rewarding and fun way to narrow your collecting scope. Whether funny or sad, all the world loves a clown!

No matter what circus items you collect, don't forget to look to the circus itself. Under today's big top, you'll find death defying feats, ferocious animal acts, graceful acrobats, and some of the best circus collectibles in town!

Several small, touring circuses pass through towns all over the country. Many of these sell snow cones in printed cups, hats that sport the circus logo, and other items prominently marked with the circus name and logo. Although it may take a while, you can even specialize by collecting items only from the circuses that you attend. For many collectors, this is the best way to keep the magic of the circus alive.

As a great showman once said, the circus is the "Greatest Show on Earth." For many collectors, collecting circus items is one of the "greatest hobbies on Earth."

Related Collectibles: carnival, fair, and expo collectibles

27

Comic Books

....

*"Fling but a stone, the giant dies.
Laugh, and be well."*
Matthew Green, 1696-1737

The first re-occurring comic strip appeared in 1892, in the *San Francisco Examiner* newspaper. The strip was called "Little Bears" but it didn't look much like the comics we know today. The Little Bears comic wasn't drawn in sequenced panels and there weren't any overhead balloons to contain the words. The antics of the Little Bears won the hearts of the *Examiner*'s readers. Other comic strips soon followed and achieved great popularity. Then, in the late 1930s, the first comic book appeared. This marked the beginning of a publishing legacy that continues to be very strong today. Comic books appeal to children and adults seeking laughter, entertainment, and enjoyment, and have been popular with collectors for a very long time.

Over the past 67 years, there have been so many comic books published, that it would be impossible to collect them all. Just keeping up with new releases is difficult, let alone collecting the older issues. So, most collectors specialize in a particular type of comic book.

Comic books with holograms, prism foil, die cuts, scratch-n-sniff, 3-D posters, or other special features are treasured, and comics with space aliens, cowboys, and famous movie and television stars have a huge following. Some collectors look for comic books featuring only specific characters. For example, some collectors only look for Tarzan comics—and, with over 200 different Tarzan comics printed by a variety of publishers, they have their work cut out for them! How about collecting Disney comic books? Mickey Mouse, Donald Duck, Pluto, and others have graced the pages of over 1,000 different comic books, and they're still being published.

Another way to specialize is to collect a single series. Most comic books in a publisher's series are numbered. With any luck, you'll choose a relatively new comic book series which might allow you to start with the first issue. Watch for new releases, and collect each of the comic books that follow in that series; however, many collectors begin with numbers 50 or 100 and build their collection from there. Before deciding what type of comic books to collect, keep in mind that the older comics are much more difficult to find and can be quite expensive.

In the 1980s, when the 1939 Action Number 1 comic book featuring Superman, sold for $1,000, it garnered national attention. Today, the same comic book would sell for several times that amount. Many other early comics are selling for very high prices as well. Even some recently published comic books are valued well above the cover price. This means that if you don't have a lot of money to invest, you'll probably want to collect the new releases. For just a few dollars, you can pick up the latest issues and watch your collection grow—and choosing an area to specialize in, might be easier than you think.

Just turn on the Saturday morning cartoons. It's likely that the most popular shows have comic books featuring their characters. The Looney Tunes, Sonic the Hedge Hog, The Simpsons and other animated stars are appearing in their own comic book series. The X-Men, Superman, Batman and other Superheros are super popular right now, so it's easy to find these new releases.

Grocery, convenience, discount, and drugstores usually carry comic books. Take a tour of the magazine or toy isles to see what comic books they carry. Ask the clerk when the new releases come in and check the shelves regularly to make sure that you keep up with whatever series you collect. Collecting comic books, especially the new ones, is fun, affordable, and you don't need much room to keep them.

Comic books can be kept in cardboard boxes, dresser drawers, or stacked on a shelf for safe keeping; however, it's a good idea to place each of them in a plastic bag. Ask a comic book dealer or store clerk where you can buy special comic-sized bags to store each issue. This will help to protect your comics from dust, moisture, and grime. You might want to use tape or tacks to hang the bag on the wall to display the front cover.

So what are you waiting for? Take a few extra dollars with you to the store and start collecting comic books!

Related Collectibles: comic strips

28

Computer
Collectibles

· ·

"The computer is no better than its program."
Elting Elmore Morison, 1909-

The abacus, a wooden rack with parallel wires strung with beads, has been used to compute numbers for over 2,000 years. Like early personal computers, its introduction was considered a milestone in technology. Unlike the abacus, however, the design, capabilities, and power of the personal computer changes so rapidly, that even a one-year-old computer is viewed by some as ancient technology. This is good news for collectors who want to preserve a bit of computing history.

The personal computing revolution began in the 1970s with the introduction of several computer "kits." The original Altar computer was a "build it yourself kit" that included everything electronics buffs needed to assemble a computer. Other kits released by Heathkit also allowed the electronic hobbyist to jump into the computer age. With "do it yourself" kits leading the way, a now familiar manufacturer came on the scene to bring the personal computer a little closer to home.

The Apple #1 computer, viewed by many as the first real personal computer, came only with a mother board. The key board and display were not included and, therefore, had to be bought separately. When all of the parts were assembled, home computing became a reality. As other electronics companies got into the computing game, many new models of computers were introduced. Names like Commodore, IBM, Timex, and others can be found on some of the earliest personal computers. Don't expect these "antiques" to look or act like any computer you have ever used, though.

Early personal computers came with as little as 16 kilobytes of memory and they took their sweet time to warm up. As much as half an hour or longer was needed for the system to come on line after the switch had been turned to "ON." Hard drives were unheard of until 1982 or 1983, and cassette tape drives were used as storage devices. Later, 5-1/4" single-sided floppy disks were used to boot up the system and to run programs from. It was a slow, laborious task using these original personal computers, but it was lightning fast compared to the old fashion manual method. These dinosaurs of the Computer Age are wonderful collectibles for anyone who enjoys old technology and has a knack for working with the hardware—but since many people and companies dispose of old computers as soon as they are replaced, it may be tricky to find them.

To get started, look in computer magazines that include advertisements for used equipment. Collectors may occasionally find old computers and parts listed in *The Computer Shopper*. Also, electronic flea markets called "Hamfests," can be good hunting grounds. Hamfests, which are sponsored by radio clubs, are held all over the country. And, there are usually at least a few people selling old computers and parts at each event. Buying secondhand computers is risky, so keep in mind the old saying "Let the buyer beware."

Usually, it isn't possible to test old computers before buying them. Many of the companies that manufactured the early models are either out of business or they don't support the old hardware anymore. This means that you may have to buy several identical computers in order to get the parts to build one working machine. Buying duplicate computers in any condition might insure that you keep replacement parts on hand. Finding collectible computers isn't the only consideration if you want to have a working collection.

Finding compatible hardware and software will also be of interest. Computers with internal hard drives sometimes come loaded with software; however, computers without hard drives, are often missing the tape or diskettes which contain the early programs. Compatible printers, plotters, and other hardware are often separated from the computers they once served.

The trick to assembling a working collection of computers is to build your collection as computers, software, printers, and plotters are found. You may have several computers for which you'll never find any software or hardware for, but that's the risk you'll have to take if you hope to build a working computer collection.

Innovation and rapidly changing technology has produced a wide variety of computer collectibles. If you're part collector and part computer whiz, then this collectible might just flip your switch!

Related Collectibles: typewriters, adding machines, slide rules

29

CUPS OR MUGS

. . . .

"Many things happen between the cup and the lip."
Robert Burton, 1577-1640

Cups and mugs made from pottery, stoneware, glass, pewter, and porcelain are among the most popular collectibles. Many people who collect these may not even realize that they do until their cupboards are bursting at the seams. It might begin with a penguin cup bought at a zoo, a mug with the name and slogan of a favorite restaurant, or a stein with a beautiful German country scene. Often, family and friends unwittingly contribute mugs from vacations, favorite sports teams, cities, or other places that they've gone. In no time at all, a cup collection has begun.

It would be impossible to know how many different cups and mugs have been made over the years. Antique, used, and new mugs are for sale almost anywhere you look. What kind of cups or mugs do you want to collect? Once you answer that question, then you can decide where to begin your search.

Many people collect cups from the places they've traveled. This makes an especially nice collection since it chronicles some of the collector's experiences. Cups or mugs bearing city, state, and country names are usually available in tourist areas. The variety of travel mugs might surprise you. Choose from a glass mug with a gold guitar and banjo positioned below "Nashville, Tenn. Music City U.S.A.," a ceramic mug with "Austin" printed in blue lettering with a red heart for the dot above the "i," or a porcelain cup with a lithograph picture of Ithaca Falls on one side and "Ithaca is Gorges" printed on the other. Just as each place has its own character, so do the souvenir cups and mugs that advertise it.

How about collecting cups from institutions? Many institutions, particularly those serving the public, have souvenir cups and mugs available for visitors and collectors. The Smithsonian Institution, for example, has many different styles to choose from including a porcelain mug with a picture of the Castle, the years it was under construction (1847-1855), and the name of the Architect (James Renwick, Jr.). Harvard University issued at least one cup in honor of their 350th Anniversary (1636-1986). Kew Gardens, The Royal Botanical Gardens of England, offers a souvenir mug with a lion, a unicorn, a crest, and several flowers printed in a stately olive green. Any of these would make a great addition to your collection. Just about every public institution will have souvenir cups that you can pick up during a visit—but what if you don't travel much? Well, there are several other options.

Cups advertising various products are often given away or sold at a nominal price with proof-of-purchase seals. Many advertising mugs are being sold in the houseware departments of discount and department stores. The Hershey company has several cups decorated with their world famous Hershey Bars and Kisses. You know Maxwell House Coffee is "Good to the last drop," but did you know that souvenir mugs can be found in some retail stores? How about those cute Campbell's Soup Kids shown on a wide-mouth mug slurping up a bowl of that "M'm! M'm! Good!" soup? Pick any product or design you like, and start building an advertising cup collection.

If you go to antique shows or shops, why not collect a bit of shaving history? Between 1865 and 1920, barber shops across America displayed shaving mugs which reflected the men that came in for a shave and a haircut. Occupational shaving mugs decorated for bricklayers, railroad men, carpenters, and other tradesmen served as a "Who's Who" of the town. Mugs showing fraternal orders or preferred sports were also the hallmark of the barber shop's mug display. Then, after World War I, when the Gillette Safety Razor was introduced, shaving mugs went by the wayside. Today, shaving mugs are highly sought after collectibles, ranging in price from $10 to several hundred.

If you're an art lover, there are cups for you, too. Some people collect handmade cups crafted by gifted artists. From the potter's wheel, the artist's kiln, or the glass blower's studio, cups, mugs, and steins of uncommon beauty are created. You can find these carefully designed pieces at craft fairs, specialty stores, and directly from the artists. The one thing to keep in mind, though, is that fine arts and crafts can be expensive. The price for handmade or decorated cups can range anywhere from $20 to $50 or more. While handmade cups and mugs make wonderful collectibles, they can require a fairly stiff investment to build a collection. For this reason, your best bet is to look for them at church bazaars, flea markets, garage sales, and other secondhand sales.

Collecting cups or mugs can be a lot of fun, many of them are affordable, and they are easy to display on shelves, hooks, or cup racks. If products, places, or artistic creations hold your interest, then collecting cups or mugs might be your cup of tea!

Related Collectibles: steins, glasses, saucers

30

Decade Collectibles

*"Each year new consuls and proconsuls are made;
but not every year is a king or poet born."*

Lucius Annaeus Florus, fl. 125

Kings and poets may not be born every year, but popular trends spring up at least that often. One way to track and preserve these trends, is to collect memorabilia that charts ten year's worth of popular culture in a decade collection. With the passing of each trend comes the next, and a collection that zeros in on a ten-year time span is certain to include some pretty interesting stuff.

Currently, we have in-line skates, pogs, action figures, and some yet unknown trends that may rise above everything else to represent this decade. In the 1980s it was the walkman, the 1970s had Mr. Bill, the 1960s was the era of the Beatles, Mr. Potato Head, and the Flintstones. The 1950s had rock-and-roll, Silly Putty, and Hula-Hoops. Pick any decade, do a little research, and you can put together a representative collection that details the styles, tastes, and technology of that era.

It should be no surprise that the easiest decade collectibles to find are from the present decade. That is to say, at the time this book was published in 1997, collectibles from the 1990s are the most readily available. Naturally, the collectibles of the current year are usually the most common. Collectibles from the next decade back, the 1980s, can be found used, but the selection and availability are somewhat less than the collectibles of the 1990s. The farther you go back, the more expensive and the harder to find the collectibles become. For that reason, we will talk mostly about assembling a collection for the current decade.

In any given decade there are dozens of areas of potential collecting interest. Music, television, toys, movies, magazines, and many other aspects of our culture reflect the time when they were popular. Decide what area you are most interested in, plan your strategy, and start collecting.

For example, in the early 1990s, country music was hotter than hot. Several country music stars saw their music rise to the top of the pop charts. By 1996, rock and alternative music crowded out the country hits of Billy Ray Cyrus and Garth Brooks on these same charts. One approach to collecting the

music of the decade might be to keep track of a particular music chart and then collect the top three, five, or ten songs of each year in the decade. A collection such as this would provide insight into the changing tastes in America's music and provide hours of entertainment.

Another area of our society that strongly reflects the times is television. The shows "Friends," "Seinfeld," "ER," "The Rosie O'Donnell Show," "The Simpsons," and others are all good examples of what the thoughts, tastes, and concerns of a particular year or decade were. One approach to collecting the decade through television might be to simply videotape and keep your favorite shows. Another approach might be to collect magazines with articles and pictures of your favorite television stars. Magazines such as *People*, *Good Housekeeping*, and others often feature the most popular television stars of the moment on the front cover.

Toys are probably second only to computers to show how rapidly things change from year to year. Cabbage Patch Kids, Teen Age Mutant Ninja Turtles, Tickle Me Elmo, Sky Dancers, Koosh, and other toys have risen to the highest heights of toy stardom, only to be replaced in an instant by another up-and-comer. A collection of the "Whos Who" of toys representing an entire decade would indeed be an interesting and fun way to mark the passage of time. Collect the most popular toys from each year or just pick and choose your favorite new playthings for a personalized decade collection.

Depending upon what decade you focus on, you can either look in retail stores or to secondhand sales to build your collection. Dollar and discount stores often have great sales on recent trends which tend to define the current decade. Items at garage sales, flea markets, and church bazaars should reflect the past 20 to 30 years. If you are interested in anything older than that, antique shows and estate auctions are your best bet.

Regardless of how you decide to collect and celebrate your chosen decade, have fun. After all, a new decade collection only comes around every ten years!

Related Collectibles: collect memorabilia from a single selected year

31

Dolls

....

"Youth is given. One must put it away like a doll in a closet, take it out and play with it only on holidays."
May Swenson, 1919-1989

Dolls have been around since the dawn of the human race; however, throughout most of their history, dolls were not regarded as toys. Over the ages, dolls have played a part in ancient religions, served as amusements for adults, and, finally, in the last century, they have become playthings for children.

Dolls are among the most human and sentimentally enduring of all playthings. They are with us when we play and sleep, they listen when we talk, and as the truest of friends, they keep our secrets. It's no wonder, then, that many collectors surround themselves with these treasured friends.

Dolls made of china, leather, plastic, rubber, straw, and wood have been the companions of the young and young at heart for many years. Add to these, composition dolls, which are made of several different materials, and there's an endless variety to collect.

Baby dolls with their round faces, tiny hands, and sleepy eyes have great appeal. Clown, Santa, railroad, and other specialty dolls are highly sought after—and there's increasing interest in celebrity dolls such as Sylvester Stallone, Michael Jackson, Donny Osmond, Princess Diana, and countless others. Modern dolls dressed in beautiful folk costumes of different countries are also quite collectible. With the wide variety of antique and new dolls available, it would be impossible to mention them all, so we'll look at some of the most popular and readily available dolls.

Born in 1959, and named after the daughter of the first owner of the Mattel Company, the Barbie doll is, without a doubt, one of the most popular dolls ever made. Limited editions and the early Barbie dolls are prized by collectors. The first few Barbie dolls are so rare, that they are estimated to be worth over $2,500. Over the years, Barbie has assembled a huge wardrobe, a tremendous variety of accessories, a wonderful list of friends, and she has enjoyed many personal achievements.

Barbie has been a teacher, a bride, an airline stewardess, a ballerina, an Olympic Gymnast, and many other things. The special Barbie dolls that speak Spanish, twist and turn, bend, and the ones that have hair that "grows," are favorites. Barbie gift sets and accessories such as the Jeep, playhouse, and camper are also very popular. Some of Barbie's best buddies such as Allan, Brad, Ken and Midge are also highly collectible. Keep in mind, though, that many of these early Barbie dolls, accessories, and friends can be quite expensive. For this reason, you might want to begin your collection with new Barbie dolls.

New Barbie dolls can be found at a toy or discount store near you. Complete with wardrobes and accessories, many Barbie dolls are priced affordably at $15 or less. Special dolls such as "My Size" Barbie, or elaborate playsets can cost $50 or more. Save your allowance and make your collecting choices carefully. Your Barbie doll collection should reflect your interests and include only the dolls and accessories that you like.

Barbie and her pals aren't the only dolls in town, though. Other collectible dolls include Cabbage Patch, Sky Dancers, and any other dolls that strikes your fancy. If you collect old or antique dolls, however, you should get a good price guide and become familiar with the types and values of dolls you're interested in.

Collecting dolls can be fun and rewarding. As you build your collection you might find yourself singing, "Oh, you beautiful doll!"

Related Collectibles: doll houses, furniture, paper dolls

ETHNIC
OR CULTURAL
Collectibles

*"Guided by my heritage of a love of beauty
and a respect for strength–
in search of my mother's garden,
I found my own."*
Alice Walker, 1944-

One of the greatest gifts that we have is our heritage. The history of our family before we were born is a rich glimpse into who we are and where we have come from. Grandparents, aunts, uncles, cousins, and family members who have come before, have helped to shape us through their ethnic and cultural practices, beliefs, and traditions. Our ethnic and cultural heritage is a connection to the past as much as it is a bridge to the future.

We can learn about our own past or the history of a people that we admire, and build an interesting collection at the same time. Ethnic or Cultural collectibles offer insight into American Indian, Irish, Japanese, Hispanic, African, and other cultures.

Asian masks, Eskimo baskets and wood carvings, German porcelain figures, Scottish wool blankets, American Indian music, African art, and countless

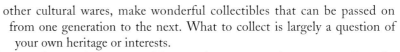

other cultural wares, make wonderful collectibles that can be passed on from one generation to the next. What to collect is largely a question of your own heritage or interests.

A second generation Mexican American might want to collect the folk songs of Mexico, handmade silver jewelry, jade statues, traditional clothing, or hand painted pottery. A collector of German decent, might be interested in German dolls, porcelain figures, or tin toys. Collectibles from India might include brass work, wood carvings, or embroidery. Every culture and ethnic group has unique wares, poetry, art, and music that would be interesting to collect.

Once you decide which ethnic or cultural group to base your collection on, you have to find the collectibles. The best way to collect ethnic and cultural collectibles is to travel to the areas where the people who created them live. This is a wonderful way to learn about the history, use, and meanings of your collectibles and to increase your understanding of the people behind them. If you aren't able to travel, seek the help of someone who does. A parent who travels for work, or grandparents who vacation abroad, may be able to bring ethnic collectibles back for you. If these options aren't possible, however, you may need to do things a little differently.

In the United States, the best place to find ethnic and cultural items for your collection is at import stores, ethnic and cultural specialty shops, and museum stores. Even in local department stores, foreign-made products can easily be found. Also, garage sales, antique and collectible stores, flea markets, and church bazaars are potential sources for collectors. But some of these items may not be true representatives of the ethnic group or culture that you are interested in. Western influences often alter the design of products that are imported for sale in to the United States. Just make sure that every ethnic and cultural collectible added to your collection is authentic enough for you.

Collecting items that reflect the heritage of any people is a noble and interesting pursuit. Fascinating and attractive displays will help you share your knowledge and admiration for the people who crafted your collectibles. It can be lots of fun as you discover the practices, traditions, and beliefs of past generations.

**Related Collectibles: national or state collectibles,
family pictures and heirlooms**

33

EVENT Collectibles

··

*"Often do the spirits
of great events stride on before the events,
And in today already walks tomorrow."*
From *Wallenstein*, 1799-1800, by Schiller

Event collectibles are one of the oldest souvenirs in the history of the human race. The coronation of King Edward VI, in 1547, may have been the first event where royal commemoratives were issued. Since the 1800s, World's Fairs and Expos have been remembered with bells, coins, cups, toys and much more. Centennials, expeditions, discoveries, and other historical events are often marked by issuing souvenirs at the time of the event or anniversary. Collectibles from very old events can be both expensive and difficult to find; however, many modern events offer an affordable variety of new collectibles

The Olympics, the Super Bowl, the World's Series and other sporting contests are long remembered through hats, T-shirts, and pennants. Renaissance Festivals, plays, concerts, and other live entertainment have playbills, posters, and autographs of the stars to mark the occasion. Political races, art shows, and museum exhibits issue buttons, bookmarks, and booklets, and the items which celebrate these events are as varied as the events themselves.

Event collectibles range from limited edition ceramics to inexpensive key chains, puzzles, and matchbooks. In fact, just about any item that has room for a picture and a date can be turned into an event collectible. Among the most popular event collectibles are plates, flags, medallions, goblets, plaques, pocketknives, and spoons. Many collectors specialize in either a particular type of event such as the World Series, or a certain kind of collectible such as spoons. If you want to collect "the next best thing to being there," however, then perhaps you should look for paper items.

Paper collectibles are possibly the most interesting type of collectibles. Books, postcards, posters, and maps often provide a history of the events. Through their words and pictures, you can almost sense what it was like to be at a particular event—even if it took place before you were born! Feel what it was like to be at the 1972 Olympic Games by reading the program. Look at pictures of fair goers riding on the Ferris Wheel at the 1964 New York State Fair. Nothing makes a collection come alive like the words and pictures of someone who was there as the event was happening.

Event collectibles can be found almost anywhere. Flea markets, garage sales, antique stores, and church bazaars are wonderful hunting grounds for collectibles from past events. Airport shops, department stores, drugstores, and street vendors often carry collectibles for current events scheduled in their cities. As you look, keep in mind that the best collectibles are in good condition and have the name, date, and location of the event printed on them. Once you decide what to collect, think about how to display your collection.

Clear off plenty of room on shelves, tables, and in cupboards to display your event collection. If you collect posters, pennants, or collectibles that can be hung, make sure you have lots of wall space. Even though you may specialize in a particular type of event collectible, you might want to look for additional items to complement your display. For example, if you collect World Series memorabilia, then add an old baseball, a mit, or a baseball bat to dress up your exhibit.

Event collectibles offer a fun and interesting way to remember life's highlights. So, select your favorite events, and go out and make your collection happen!

Related Collectibles: city, state, and national collectibles

34

Eyeglasses

··

*"For I dipp'd into the future, far as human eye could see,
Saw the Vision of the world, and all the wonder that would be . . . "*

Alfred, Lord Tennyson, 1809-1892

"**F**ar as human eye could see," became even farther after the first eye-glasses appeared in the thirteenth century. Although no one is certain who invented glasses, or spectacles as they are sometimes called, the Englishman Roger Bacon often receives the credit. Even though their purpose has remained constant over the past 800 years, eyeglass design has varied greatly. Each year, designers introduce hundreds of new examples of fashionable eye-wear. Whether for style, sport, or just to help us see better, the diversity is amazing. It's this variety which makes spectacles an interesting and fun collectible.

In the 1970s, pop-singer Elton John became famous for the wild and sometimes weird glasses which he wore on stage. Oversized, gaudy, and sometimes battery-powered, John's glasses attracted attention. Possibly because of his example, the styles of everyday glasses became an avenue for artistic expression and personal taste. Small or large frames, round or square lenses, sequined or glittered, eyeglasses have almost become an art form—and every color in the rainbow has been used to decorate the plastic, alloy, or metal frames. Tinted lenses, logo-embedded temples, and other design features have increased the variety of eye-wear considerably over the past ten years. This means that anyone who is interested in collecting glasses, has an amazing assortment of collectibles to choose from.

It's probably safe to say that there aren't many people who *collect* eyeglasses; however, given that half of all Americans wear glasses and 95% of adults over 45 years of age wear them for reading or close work, it's a good bet that you'll need them at some point in your life—so why not collect them?

To begin a collection of spectacles, start with your family and friends. Chances are, they have several pairs of eyeglasses stashed in cabinets, tucked away in drawers, or stacked on shelves. Depending upon how trendy their original owners were, the spectacle collection you assemble might be a showcase of styles covering the past several years. Once you've asked everyone you know to contribute their old glasses to your collection, then start looking elsewhere.

Garage sales, auctions, estate sales, and other secondhand sales are good places to look for used spectacles. Old, or very unique glasses sometimes turn up at antique shops, flea markets, and vintage clothing stores. If you're really lucky, a friendly eye doctor or optometrist might give you some of their discarded glasses for your collection. Be aware that some service groups collect used glasses that are in good condition to pass on

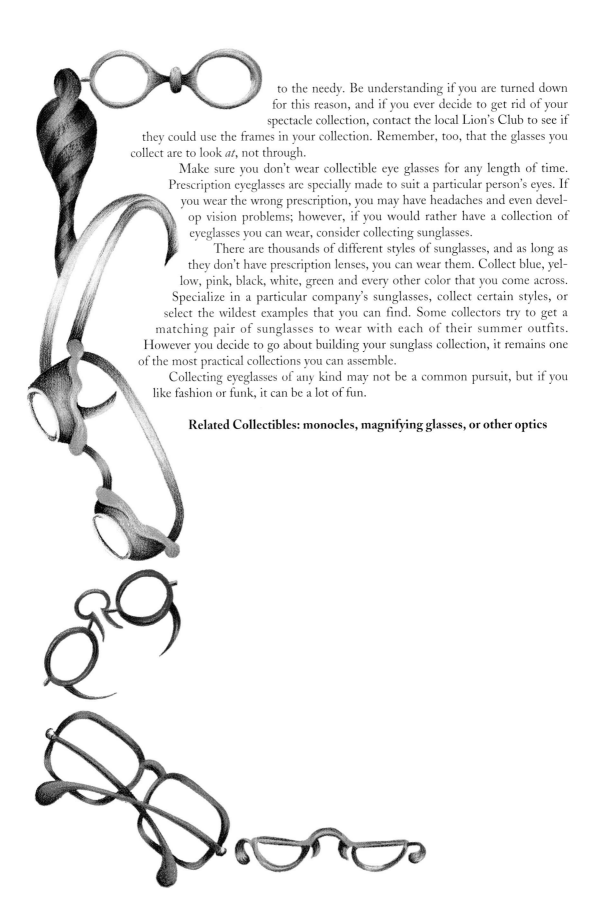

to the needy. Be understanding if you are turned down for this reason, and if you ever decide to get rid of your spectacle collection, contact the local Lion's Club to see if they could use the frames in your collection. Remember, too, that the glasses you collect are to look *at*, not through.

Make sure you don't wear collectible eye glasses for any length of time. Prescription eyeglasses are specially made to suit a particular person's eyes. If you wear the wrong prescription, you may have headaches and even develop vision problems; however, if you would rather have a collection of eyeglasses you can wear, consider collecting sunglasses.

There are thousands of different styles of sunglasses, and as long as they don't have prescription lenses, you can wear them. Collect blue, yellow, pink, black, white, green and every other color that you come across. Specialize in a particular company's sunglasses, collect certain styles, or select the wildest examples that you can find. Some collectors try to get a matching pair of sunglasses to wear with each of their summer outfits. However you decide to go about building your sunglass collection, it remains one of the most practical collections you can assemble.

Collecting eyeglasses of any kind may not be a common pursuit, but if you like fashion or funk, it can be a lot of fun.

Related Collectibles: monocles, magnifying glasses, or other optics

35

FACTS

....

"Now, what I want is Facts.
Teach these boys and girls
Nothing but Facts. Facts alone
are wanted in life. Plant nothing else, and root out
everything else."
Charles Dickens, 1812-1870

The world is full of fun facts to know and share: Ice cream sundaes first appeared in Ithaca, New York in 1897. President Millard Fillmore married his schoolteacher. The safety pin was patented in 1849 by Walter Hunt. Even when you least expect it, a fact will jump right out at you. Your dad might tell you that golf tees were patented in 1899; your mom might remind you that earmuffs were invented by Chester Greenwood in 1873, in Farmington, Maine; or your teacher might report that the first state board of education was established in Massachusetts in 1837. Facts are everywhere, and they are among the most affordable collectible.

Keep your facts on 3" x 5" cards, in a notebook, or in a computer database, and all you'll pay for is storing the facts. Unless you photocopy the information, the facts shouldn't cost you a dime. In addition to being inexpensive, facts are very useful. Quiz your friends and family, add flavor to your essays and school reports, or just revel in your newfound knowledge. For a broad-based collection, keep track of any facts that interest you, or specialize in information about selected topics.

Collect facts about schools or education. The first swimming school was started in Boston in 1827; the first gymnasium was built in Northampton, Massachusetts, in 1825; and the first Kindergarten in the United States was opened by Mrs. Carl Schurz in New York City in 1856. To bring your school facts a little closer to home, make a list of all of the colleges in your state, the dates they were opened, the programs they offer, or the "famous" people who graduated from them. In no time at all, you'll know a great deal about the history of education in your state. This is just one option, though. There are many, many different types of facts to collect.

You can collect facts about inventions: The ice cream freezer was invented in 1848, the Slinky was created by engineer Richard James in 1943, and since Johnson & Johnson introduced the Band-Aid in 1921, over 205 billion of them have been sold. Research patents and keep track of the patent dates and details of your favorite products; keep a list of product anniversaries (i.e., Lincoln Logs celebrated 80 years in 1996); create a list of achievements for your favorite inventor.

How about collecting some "pop" facts? Did you know that Van Buren, Indiana, is the popcorn capital of the world? That Native Americans used popcorn to decorate corsages, headdresses, and necklaces—or that popcorn expands about 45 times its size when it's popped? Well, if you collected facts about this popular snack food, you probably would. Pick a food or product that you like and find out more about it than just how to use it.

If you're looking for more meaning in the facts you collect, then grab a dictionary and dig a little deeper. At the end of a word, when you see "ology," it means "science or study." For example, the "entomo" in entomology means insect; therefore, "entomology" is the study of insects—and vexillology is the study of flags, seismology is the study of earthquakes, ichthyology is the study of fish, and audiology is the study of hearing. There are many words that end in "ology" and a collection of them would make an interesting study.

If you want to collect facts that are a little more on the wild side, how about facts about animals? You know that a group of sheep are called a flock and that a bunch of bees buzzing together is called a swarm, but do you know what other groups of animals are called? It's a barren of mules, a crash of rhinoceroses, an ostentation of peacocks, a troop of monkeys, a parliament of owls, and a dray of squirrels. Finding this information requires pulling out a big heavy dictionary and doing a bit of research, but it will impress your classmates, enlarge your vocabulary, and make for great reading. Even if you already collect something else, collecting facts can be part of your hobby.

Whether you collect insects, toys, books, stamps or just about anything else, you can collect facts about your collectibles. Learn about the insects in your collection—what they eat, where they live, how many species there are, and anything else you can learn about them from reading or talking with an expert. If you collect toys, find out about the toy's history, the company that makes them, how they are made, and any other scrap of information you can dig up. Learning about your collectibles and keeping the facts close at hand is a fun way to get the most out of your hobby.

Collecting facts is a great reason to spend Saturday mornings at the local library. If you enjoy a little research, learning new things, and keeping a record of them, then get the facts, collector—just the facts!

Related Collectibles: important dates in history, reference books

80

Fishing Gear

*"A bad day fishing is better
than a good day at work!"*
Author unknown, bumper sticker

There's nothing better than a warm sunny day by the lake with a cold soda in one hand, and a fishing pole in the other. For thousands of years, fishing has been an important means of putting food on the table, but it wasn't until the first person fished for fun rather than for survival, that it became a sport. Over the years, fishing has become the great American pastime—and, as the sport developed, so did the technology.

The production of fishing tackle is one of the oldest industries known to man. Traced back to prehistoric times, early fishing gear consisted of harpoons with bone, antler, or stone points for spearing fish. This method of fishing required a sharp aim, a quick hand, and strength. The difficulty of spear fishing meant that a few, quick fishermen would have to supply the entire village with fish. What was needed was a way to make fishing accessible to everyone, so that the catch could be increased.

Around 12,000 to 9000 B.C., curved hooks fashioned from stone, shell, or bone, were tied to the end of a string and concealed with bait. Anyone who could cast a line could catch a fish. Later, metal barbed hooks, lures, flies, casting reels, rods, and other technology furthered fishing not only as a sport, but also as an area for collectors. In fact, fishing collectibles are becoming so popular that collector's groups are springing up all over the country.

Among the most popular fishing collectibles are the lures. Lures are man-made baits, crafted to resemble minnows, eels, frogs, and other natural fish foods. While the number of different kinds of lures is mind boggling, they can be divided into two distinct groups. The two basic kinds of lures are spoons and plugs. Spoons, which have been around the longest, are polished metal strips. Designed to look like small swimming fish, spoons are rather plain and, therefore, not as popular with collectors. Plugs, on the other hand, come in a variety of colors and shapes, and they are favorites among both fishermen and collectors.

81

Multi-colored plugs made of wood, metal, plastic, and just about every other kind of material imaginable, have caught the attention of collectors. Names like Chub Pollywiggle, Crab Wiggler, Nemo Bass Bait, Shiner, Musky Mouse and others are at the top of the collectible list. Old wooden lures with glass eyes are among the most treasured, but the general rule is: The more interesting the plug's design, the more highly it is sought after. Prices for plugs can range from a few cents at garage sales to hundreds of dollars at antique shows—so it's best to start fishing for lures where the price is right.

Hardly anyone ever throws away tackle boxes full of fishing gear, so first check with family and friends to see if they have any lures stashed away in their basements or attics. This is the best way to collect older lures which may have been passed down from one generation to another. Another great source for fishing collectibles is garage sales. Much of the tackle that's sold at neighborhood sales is modestly priced, and many great lures can turn up. While you're looking for lures, don't overlook other fine fishing collectibles.

Brass, stainless, and even some plastic fishing reels have become highly sought after because of their interesting designs or styles. Also, fishing rods which have been made of wood, split bamboo, plastics, and state-of-the-art metals, can make a great addition to any fishing collection. Fishing creels, nets, stringers, hand-tied flies, and other gear is of interest to collectors. What would a collection of fishing collectibles be if it didn't give you bragging rights?

For collectors, sharing the catch is almost as much fun as reeling it in—and the options for displaying the catch are as varied as the collectibles themselves. For example, probably the nicest way to display lures is to attach them to a solid cloth backing and frame them in a glass-covered shadow box. This becomes a fairly permanent display, so make sure you'll never want to trade or sell the ones you frame. For a less costly alternative, hang a cork board on the wall and hook the lures into the cork. If wall space is at a premium, then, with your parents' permission, "hook" the lures on a curtain rod in your room. Fishing reels can be displayed on shelves, cupboards, or on tables, and while commercially manufactured fishing pole racks are nice, a sheet of peg board with some hooks works just as well.

Collecting fishing collectibles is a great way to enjoy the sport in between fishing seasons. If the sight of the lure, the feel of the pole, and the thrill of the catch makes you happy, just put up a sign that says "Gone fishing . . . for collectibles."

Related Collectibles: fishing advertisements

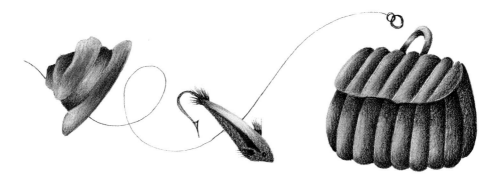

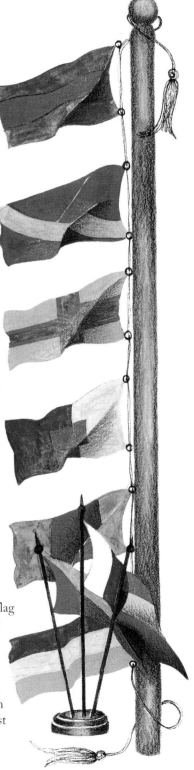

Flags

·····················

" 'Shoot, if you must, this old gray head,
But spare your country's flag,' she said."
John Greenleaf Whittier, 1807-1892

A flag is a piece of colored fabric that serves as a symbol or signaling device. It can show patriotism, announce the winner at the finish line, or it may mean that a collector is nearby. Many collectors are fascinated with the history and use of these versatile banners.

Flags are used to convey many things—loyalty, hope, protection, honor, victory, challenge and more are communicated through flags. Patriots swell with national pride while displaying their country's flag. Ships and the ports they sailed from are identified by flags flown from the top of the mast. Racing fans cheer and shout as the winner is waved in by the checkered flag. With so many uses, it isn't surprising there are thousands of different flag designs.

Early American flag makers took great artistic license in creating the first flags. The Flag Act of 1777 wasn't very specific about the size or design of the U.S. Flag. Older U.S. Flags range in size from as small as 5" x 7" to 104" x 247" or larger. Size isn't the only standard, though, which varied in early American flag making.

A variety of star patterns was used to create an imaginative assortment of collectible banners. Although flags with 11 to 47 stars were made, these early examples can be both expensive and difficult to find; however, there are other options for the aspiring flag collector.

Machine-sewn U.S. flags with 48 to 49 stars can be found at military, civil war, used book stores, and antique shows. Even flea markets and garage sales occasionally feature one of these affordable prizes. If, however, you're interested in building a flag collection with a broader interest, look for table-top flags.

In the United States, 4" x 6" table-top flags are available for many large cities and for each state. These collectible miniature flags can be found at flag stores or at shops which are frequented by tourists such as airport stores, gift stores that specialize in particular states or cities, and at some resorts. Table-top flags are affordable and they are among the easiest flags to find and display—they're available for many foreign countries, too.

There are three basic ways to get foreign table-top flags: Collect them when you travel abroad, trade flags with foreign collectors, or buy them from flag stores or manufacturers. While the first two options may have the most

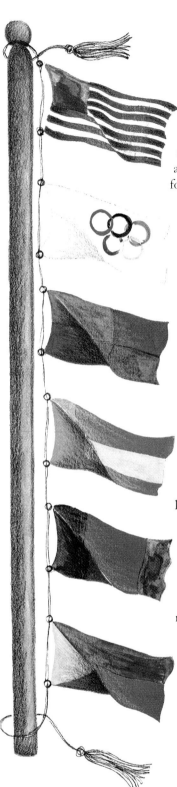

appeal, buying collectible flags from flag stores and manufacturers is the most efficient way to build a collection—but if city, state, and national flags don't interest you, then specialty flags just might.

There are many different types of specialty flags to collect, including signal flags. Railroads once relied on signal flags so that station workers could communicate with the engine driver. Ships of all kinds employed signal flags for calls to action, to convey status, and for ceremonial occasions. Although sending a long message with signal flags may be cumbersome, it is possible. There are twenty-six different flags representing each letter of the alphabet. A collection of these colorful flags would make a wonderful and interesting display. Signal flags can be found at local marinas, flag stores, or at maritime museums.

Another related area of collecting is military flags. Each branch of the military has numerous flags for signaling, identification, and ceremonial purposes. For example, each Army Battalion flies a unique flag, and each unit in the battalion has a smaller flag of its own. The Navy, Air Force, Marines, and the Coast Guard all have flags with special meanings. Military flags can be found at surplus stores, often at very reasonable prices—and there are non-military specialty flags as well.

Many civilian organizations and businesses fly their own flags. For example, each team in the National Football League has a flag of their own. A collection of these specialty flags would have cross-over appeal for the flag buff who spends Sundays watching football. Many colleges and universities fly flags with their official emblems, and some businesses have corporate flags which mark their location and promote their enterprise. McDonalds, is one example of an American business that hoists a corporate flag. All you have to do is look, and you'll see flags almost everywhere!

Many factors influence the price of a flag. The age, scarcity, artistic merit, condition, and whether a flag is hand- or machine-made all have a bearing. If you begin to buy expensive flags, look for a good price guide or a helpful dealer and become familiar with current values.

Collecting flags is fun and it should result in a collection that you enjoy looking at—so if you like to watch flags flap in the breeze, this challenging and interesting collectible might just be for you!

Related Collectibles: flag poles, finials, other collectibles with flags printed on them

38

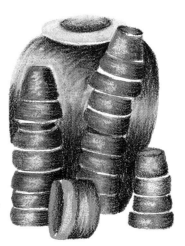

Flowerpots
....

*"Daffodils, that come before the swallow dares, and take
the winds of March with beauty."*
William Shakespeare, 1564-1616

Fragrant geraniums, golden daffodils, and a rainbow of tulips colored pink, yellow, and purple, can brighten up an entire room. Before these beautiful flowers can live inside, though, they need a home. A multi-colored glazed pot, a yellow cat planter, or any one of a thousand different flowerpots will enhance the beauty of these living treasures. Flowerpots make nice, practical collections that can add beauty to your room, or to the whole house!

Flowerpots are made from many different kinds of materials. Clay, porcelain, brass, cast iron, and tin have all been fashioned into a variety of flowerpots. Among the most collectible are the figural pots or planters.

Figural planters come in elegant, interesting, and amusing shapes. A swallowtail butterfly seemingly glides through the air as ivy grows between its planter wings. Two intertwined geometric shapes hold the soil that blankets the bluebonnets that will flower in the spring. A white-faced clown planter has a cactus growing out of his hat. Cats, elephants, cars, birds, trains, frogs, and just about any thing you can think of has, at one time or another, been fashioned into a planter. The variety, availability, and affordability of planters make them an appealing collectible, and the planters which are no longer being made are often the most interesting.

Look for figural planters at garage sales, flea markets, church bazaars, thrift stores, or at almost any secondhand sales. They turn up frequently and are often priced at one dollar or less; however, before adding a planter to your collection, make sure you inspect it very thoroughly. Hairline cracks, chips, discoloration, or other damage not only diminishes the looks of the planter, but it might also render it useless. Good condition is just as important as a good price when it comes to figural planters.

If figural planters aren't "serious" enough for you, though, how about a collection of artware planters? Artware flowerpots are skillfully shaped on a potter's wheel. Many of these earthenware pots are beautifully hand-decorated with special glazes. For this reason, artware pots are often one-of-a-kind pieces. When a collection of artware flowerpots are assembled, they reflect the interests and tastes of the collector, making a truly "personal" collection.

Artware flowerpots can easily be found at arts and craft shows, gift stores, and in other specialty shops. They do tend to be expensive when purchased at retail or art shows, so keep an eye out for them at secondhand sales where you will pay only a fraction of their original price.

Collecting flowerpots and planters is a neat hobby. If it compliments your interest in houseplants or gardens, your collection is sure to grow!

Related Collectibles: flower vases

GAMES

· ·

" 'The game is done! I've won, I've won!'
Quoth she, and whistles thrice."
Samuel Taylor Coleridge, 1772-1834

Now, here's a collectible you can have a lot of fun with! A game collection and a few friends can turn a dreary, rainy day into the most entertaining time of the week. Pull out the Monopoly board and see who can break the bank, test your command of the English language with Scrabble, or shuffle the deck and deal up a game of Uno. Even if you don't play them much, collecting games is just plain fun!

Before you grab your allowance and head out in search of games, you should decide what *kind* of games you want to collect. There are almost as many types of games as there are collectors. Some collectors specialize in games of chance, while others look for games requiring strategy or physical skill. There are collectors who specialize in certain topics such as baseball, geography, or military, and some collectors are even more narrowly focused.

There are collectors who specialize in a single, particular game. Ancient games such as Parcheesi and Chess have been manufactured for a very long time in many different countries. Hundreds of different versions of these old friends have been manufactured over the years, making them very appealing to collectors. For example, a Chess collection might include several different sets with pieces made out of plastic, metal, stone, wood, and glass, or the collection

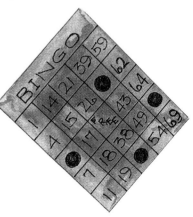

might include special issue sets with the standard pieces being replaced by cartoon characters, animals, or famous people. Unique playing boards made of glass, marble, wood, or other appealing material might also entice a Chess collector to pick up the set. If this approach isn't for you, how about games from the small screen?

Another popular category of games is television game shows. The "home" versions of Jeopardy, Wheel of Fortune, Password, the Dating Game, and other televised competitions can make an interesting collection. For just a few dollars, recent releases can often be found at garage sales, flea markets, and other second-hand sales. It's likely your friends and family will already know how to play!

To give your game collection a little more personality, you can take another approach. Games that feature well-known personalities or cartoon characters are also highly collectible. Captain Kangaroo, Barney, Daniel Boone, Johnny Quest, the Grinch, Mickey Mouse, and many other personalities appear in a variety of board and card games. Syndicated programs such as "Charlie's Angels," "M*A*S*H," "Dallas," "Columbo," and "Mork & Mindy" have also been featured. Even movies such as *Mary Poppins, James Bond,* and *ET the Extra-Terrestrial* have been seen in the game isles. These types of games are great to collect, but they can be difficult to find. Competition from character or television collectors is fierce, and not many of the older games withstood the rigorous play of their young owners.

When buying used games, make sure that each game is complete and in good condition. Look for the instruction booklet or on the box lid to find an inventory of the game pieces or parts. Unless a game is very old or rare, you might want to think twice before buying one that's missing pieces.

One exception to this rule is if you are collecting games primarily for the artwork on the box-top. Detailed lithographs on the front of old game boxes are highly collectible. Often, the artwork is enough reason for some collectors to purchase them (When the artwork is attractive, the box-top or board can be set on a shelf or hung on a wall to be displayed). Low-tech games aren't the only kind that collectors are searching for, though.

Electronic games such as hand-held football, golf, or arcade-style games are popular. Video and computer games are also worth considering; however, whenever these games are bought in used-condition, they should be tested to make sure they work.

Whether you specialize in games of chance, physical skill, or strategy, building a collection isn't child's play . . . but it is a lot of fun!

Related Collectibles: playing cards, toys

Greeting Cards

....

*"A strange volume of real life
in the daily packet of the postman.
Eternal love and instant payment!"*

Douglas Jerrold, 1803-1857

Today, if you want to send your thoughts or emotions to someone, you don't even have to write the message yourself. Just go to the greeting card isle in almost any store and choose from a mind-boggling selection of machine-made sentiments. Friendship, congratulations, sympathy, and other heart-felt feelings come pre-packaged.

Christmas, Halloween, Easter and other recognized holidays are celebrated every year with millions of cards that are exchanged each season. Even though you might not think of sending greeting cards for Memorial, Flag, or Labor Day, there are cards available to help get you into the spirit. Any of the cards created in honor of these special days are potential collectibles, and the variety and number of greeting cards available promises a life-long pursuit.

Most collectors specialize in a particular type of greeting card. For example, valentines, which first appeared in the 1700s, are quite popular. Valentine cards feature a variety of subjects—including advertising, transportation, music, movie characters, cartoons, and other topics. Many Valentine's Day card collectors are interested in the older examples, and they might even specialize in a specific topic. For example, elaborate valentines from the Victorian era featuring angels or cupids are among the most collectible. These cards frequently show up at antique and paper shows and sell for $10 and up.

Pop-up or three-dimensional greeting cards are also highly prized. These wonderful examples of human ingenuity date from the 1860s to the present. Open up the card, and a paper sculpture springs out at you. Buildings, animals, angels, and many other things have been featured in pop-up cards; however, these cards can be difficult to find in good condition and they can cost $25 or more. It might make more sense to begin with new cards which can be found at greeting card stores for $5 or less. If music is more to your liking, how about collecting cards that serenade you?

Musical cards with battery-operated tunes have been available for about the past twenty years. Open the card to hear music that matches the mood of the card's message. Most card shops carry at least a few examples of these musical greetings. The good news for collectors is that some of them are being designed so that you can replace their tiny battery. This prolongs the life of the card both as entertainment and as a collectible. If you want to buy one of these musical greetings from a retail shop, expect to pay $2 to $7. Not a bad price for a collectible that can keep on giving long after the party balloons and presents have been taken away.

Another way to specialize is to look for greeting cards which feature your hobby or other interests. If you love horses, rainbows or trains, there are probably a lot of different cards that reflect these interests. If medicine, sports, or teaching appeals to you as a future occupation, it's likely that you can find several cards with these themes. In fact, nearly every facet of life has been featured in, and even poked fun at, in greeting cards. It isn't that difficult, by the way, to find cards for your collection.

Certainly, you can buy brand new cards at grocery, department, variety, gift, and greeting card stores—but you can also find older cards at garage sales, auctions, antique shops, and flea markets. Sometimes, these secondhand sales are the best way to find interesting cards that reflect the styles and trends of the times that they were printed—and some of these treasures make wonderful decorations.

Greeting cards can be displayed by setting them on shelves or tables, or they can be framed and hung on the wall. You can buy several inexpensive photo frames to put your cards in, and then rotate them for an ever-changing display.

Whatever direction your greeting card collection takes you, have fun and happy collecting!

Related Collectibles: postcards

41

HATS

····················

"In the beginning, Bartholomew Cubbins didn't have five hundred hats. He had only one hat. It was an old one that had belonged to his father and his father's father before him. It was probably the oldest and the plainest hat in the whole Kingdom of Didd, where Bartholomew Cubbins lived. But Bartholomew liked it   especially because of the feather that always pointed straight up in the air."

From *The 500 Hats of Bartholomew Cubbins,*
by Dr. Seuss, 1904-1991

Bartholomew Cubbins didn't set out to collect hats, but before he knew it, he had taken 500 of them off his head. For some collectors, their hat collection grows almost as quickly as Bartholomew's did. When other people find out that you're collecting hats, you'll start getting them as presents. You'll find them under the Christmas tree, in the mail, and whenever a friend is cleaning out the attic—and that's about the best way to start collecting hats.

Hats have been around since at least 2300 B.C., when the early Egyptians wore elaborate headdresses. Gold, woven fabrics studded with jewels and feathers were worn by the very wealthy in ancient society. Since that time, the shapes, styles, and even the material used to make hats has changed. Wood, metal, straw, fur, and fabric are used to create hats for a variety of purposes.

In the 1897 issue of the Sears and Roebuck Catalogue, the number of hats offered for sale were staggering. A variety of men's styles including Crusher, Railroad, U.S.A. Cavalry, Sportsman, Mustang, Planter, Fancy Golf Caps, Straw, Conductor, Yacht Caps, and others could be bought for as little as twenty-one cents. Women also had an overwhelming amount of millinery choices. Delicate fabrics with ribbon, lace, artificial fruits, and silk flowers were used to make dainty hats and bonnets. Styles like the Florence, the Swell Evangeline, Star Shaped, and the Lace Straw Bonnet adorned the heads of the most prominent Victorian women. Although hats might not be as popular today as they were back then, there's still a variety of hats for a collector to choose from.

There are hundreds of different types of hats, and chances are the people in your family have a dozen or more tucked away in their closets. The cowboy hat that belonged to Uncle Floyd, the top hat that dad wore when he married your mom, the Easter bonnet that little sister fussed about, and the toy fireman's hat that brother played with are all good candidates for your collection. Look around, ask family members if they have any hats to spare, and then take your search to friends and to the stores.

Hat collectors sometimes specialize in a particular type of hat. For example, straw, cowboy, and ski hats come in enough colors and styles to keep a collector busy for quite a while. Bonnets, fedoras, tops, and other fancy hats suit collectors who prefer the dressy look. If none of these hats appeal to you, however, how about collecting one of today's most common styles—baseball caps.

Take a walk through the local mall, the park, or down the street. You're likely to spot them everywhere. Team emblems, company logos, cartoon characters, humorous sayings, and more decorate baseball caps. Men, women, boys, and girls all sport these brimmed billboards, and these colorful caps are comfortable, affordable, and practical. They shade our eyes from the sun and keep dust out of our hair. With many different caps to choose from, baseball caps are easy to find.

Collect baseball caps from wherever you travel, the events you attend, or with the emblems of the products you use. Look for hats featuring your favorite sports teams, colleges, or heroes—or you can do what one collector in Oregon did . . . he collected every baseball cap he found until his drawers, closets, and rooms were packed full of them.

Regardless of whether you collect baseball or some other type of hat, you can find them at retail stores, garage sales, auctions, flea markets, and church bazaars. If you collect very old hats, then antique and vintage clothing stores might be your best bet. Keep in mind that if you buy used hats, you'll probably want to have them cleaned before wearing them.

After you have a few caps, you'll need to decide how to display and store your collection. Hang hats on hooks, hat racks, or set them on shelves to be admired. Wear them on holidays, for parties, or to play dress up. After all, collecting hats is fun! If you wind up collecting as many hats as Bartholomew did, my hat's off to you!

Related Collectibles: hat boxes, hat bands, hat pins

42

Holiday Collectibles

....

*"He capers, he dances, he has eyes
of youth, he writes verses, he
speaks holiday, he smells April and May."*
William Shakespeare, 1564-1616

From New Year's Day to New Year's Eve, the most wonderful times of the year are the holidays. They are an excuse to visit family, an incentive to travel far distances to be with friends, and an invitation to enjoy the best food of the season. Holidays are a time to honor those who made sacrifices for the rest of us, and a time to give to others. Without a doubt, the holidays are among the most treasured of times. If the holidays hold a special place in your heart, too, then you might want to collect the trimmings of these celebrated days.

Almost every national holiday comes with decorations or other trimmings. For example, New Year's Eve has party hats and noisemakers, Valentine's Day is known for cards and heart-shaped boxes of candy, Saint Patrick's Day has four leaf clovers and leprechauns, and bunnies and chicks frolic down the store isles to help us celebrate Easter. Collect any of these and you'll be ready to celebrate!

Most collectors specialize in a particular holiday—that way they can focus their efforts and money on building the best seasonal collection possible. One holiday which has become very popular with collectors is Halloween.

The list of Halloween collectibles is endless. Scary skeletons, horrible monster masks, noisemakers, and spooky decorations are highly collectible. Almost anything orange with black cats, jack-o'-lanterns, spiders, ghosts, or goblins is fair game. Halloween postcards, candy bowls, and lanterns are prized by collectors. If Halloween collectibles frighten you, though, how about something a little more jolly?

Christmas is perhaps the most collectible holiday. Ornaments, decorations, figurines, lights, stockings, cookie cutters, and other trimmings bring seasons greetings. Santa Claus, snowmen, elves, reindeer, and other traditional symbols are collected along with anything that has a wreath, candy cane, or star. Christmas ducks, bunnies, deer, geese, bears, and squirrels have expanded this collecting field even more. Also, green, red, gold, and silver can turn "miscellaneous stuff" into the "Christmas stuff" that collectors want. If you aren't dreaming of a white Christmas, or a collection to celebrate it, then collect another holiday.

Independence Day, President's Day, Memorial Day, Flag Day, and Labor Day are rung in with the help of buttons, banners, and flags. All of these special days roll in with a healthy supply of seasonal collectibles.

Holiday collectibles are everywhere. Grocery, department, specialty, and even convenience stores offer seasonal collectibles. The trick to building a good holiday collection at affordable prices, is to go to these retail stores the day after the holiday. This way you can take advantage of sales of up to 70% off. Although it might be difficult to sit back and let that special day pass you by, it's a strategy that will help your collection grow more quickly.

For older collectibles, antique stores, flea markets, garage sales, and other secondhand sales stock holiday trimmings year-round. Although older collectibles are popular, building a collection this way requires caution. Many holiday collectibles, especially antiques, can be overpriced or very expensive. If you collect these early holiday pieces, consult a good price guide or find a knowledgeable dealer who's willing to help you learn about current values.

Gathering holiday collectibles is one of the most celebrated hobbies. It can be a lot of fun and for at least one day each year, you'll have the most popular collection on the block!

Related Collectibles: event collectibles

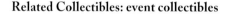

93

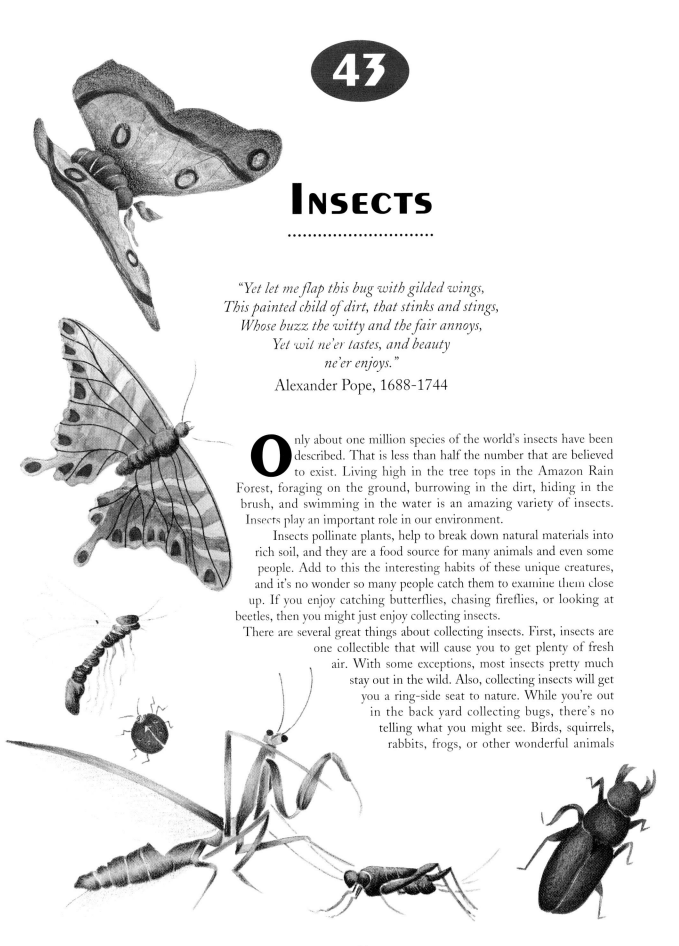

43

INSECTS

....

"Yet let me flap this bug with gilded wings,
This painted child of dirt, that stinks and stings,
Whose buzz the witty and the fair annoys,
Yet wit ne'er tastes, and beauty
ne'er enjoys."

Alexander Pope, 1688-1744

O nly about one million species of the world's insects have been described. That is less than half the number that are believed to exist. Living high in the tree tops in the Amazon Rain Forest, foraging on the ground, burrowing in the dirt, hiding in the brush, and swimming in the water is an amazing variety of insects. Insects play an important role in our environment.

Insects pollinate plants, help to break down natural materials into rich soil, and they are a food source for many animals and even some people. Add to this the interesting habits of these unique creatures, and it's no wonder so many people catch them to examine them close up. If you enjoy catching butterflies, chasing fireflies, or looking at beetles, then you might just enjoy collecting insects.

There are several great things about collecting insects. First, insects are one collectible that will cause you to get plenty of fresh air. With some exceptions, most insects pretty much stay out in the wild. Also, collecting insects will get you a ring-side seat to nature. While you're out in the back yard collecting bugs, there's no telling what you might see. Birds, squirrels, rabbits, frogs, or other wonderful animals might make an appearance. Finally, once you have a few basic pieces of equipment, there really isn't much cost involved.

The basic equipment needed to begin collecting insects shouldn't cost much more than $20. First, you'll need a net to catch flying insects. You can either go to a nature store and pick up a child-sized net, or you can check a toy store to see if they have one that will work. Look for netting that has fairly small holes so the tiny bugs won't escape. Next, you'll need a good insect field guide which should be available at any good bookstore. This valuable reference will help you identify the insects that you catch, determine the best means of preserving them, and provide interesting information about habitat, behavior, and distribution.

There are many fascinating insects that you can probably collect right in your own backyard. Leaf cutting ants that take bits of plants back to their burrows to grow fungus for food, ant lions that build cone-shaped pits in the sand to trap their prey, dragonflies who carve out and defend their territory, or beautiful butterflies that feed on the nectar of flowers and pollinate them as they feast, are but a few of the insects you might want to collect. Before deciding what kind to collect, keep in mind that there are many different ways to preserve and store insects, some methods work only for certain types of insects.

Generally speaking, soft-body insects such as mayflies, stoneflies, and various larvae, are stored in vials or jars filled with some type of preservative. Rubbing alcohol or another preservative recommended in the field guide, and approved of by your parents, should work fine. For hard-body insects such as beetles, dragonflies, or butterflies, pinning them works best. For pinning, you'll need a box with a sheet of Styrofoam on the bottom and some insect pins. The field guide should provide information on pinning and display techniques.

Insects are fascinating creatures and collecting them is an interesting hobby. Perhaps you should try it to see what all the buzz is about!

Related Collectibles: other nature collectibles

Jewelry

....

*"Kissing your hand may make you feel very, very good,
but a diamond and sapphire bracelet lasts forever."*

Anita Loos, 1893-1981

Jewelry making is one of the oldest crafts in recorded history. The first jewelry was probably made from rocks, seeds, feathers, seashells, and other natural materials, and over time, jewelry has been crafted from metal, plastic, wood, glass, and many other man-made and natural substances. The only limits to the variety of jewelry has been technology and the imagination of the artist. This makes jewelry an extraordinary collectible.

Very few collectors fill their jewelry boxes with diamonds and emeralds set in expensive gold or platinum settings. In fact, most collectors look for inexpensive trinkets and costume jewelry. Collectors select jewelry for its personal appeal, artistic merit, or sentimental value. Jewelry preference is a personal choice, one that leads many collectors to specialize.

Some collectors look for a particular type of jewelry such as bracelets, rings or lockets—while others search for jewelry based on a certain subject. For example, a collector who specializes in floral jewelry might have necklaces, earrings, or pins decorated with flowers of all kinds. Some collectors only add jewelry made out of silver, gold, Bakelite, or birth stones to their collection; however, one of the most interesting jewelry collectibles are brooches.

Brooches dating from the 1920s through the 1950s are treasured by many collectors. These decorative pins come in a variety of materials including metal, plastic, glass, and wood, and the number of subjects featured on brooches is unlimited. There are heart, cameo, flower, ribbon, fruit, animal, and portrait brooches. Also, celebrate the seasons with brooches adorned with fall leaves, pumpkins, Christmas bells, or flags. Express your interests by wearing brooches with paint brushes, books, bowling pins and balls, insects or anything else that strikes your fancy. You can enjoy your collection, and share it with others, by wearing a different brooch every day.

Our passion for these personal decorations has lead to jewelry being sold in gift, department, and other specialty stores. You can even find jewelry for sale in grocery, convenience, and toy stores. If you decide to collect old jewelry, scour garage sales, flea markets, and auctions for interesting pieces at bargain prices. Antique stores and estate sales also have fine antique jewelry, but it can be quite expensive. Finally, don't forget to let your family and friends know that you're a jewelry collector. They may have a piece or two to contribute to your collection.

Collecting jewelry is fun, and it can give you a lifetime of beautiful things to wear!

Related Collectibles: watches, decorative buttons

Jigsaw Puzzles

*"Mr. Kane was a man who got everything he wanted,
and then lost it. Maybe Rosebud was something he couldn't get or something he lost.
Anyway, it wouldn't have explained anything. I don't think any word can explain a
man's life. No, I guess Rosebud is just a piece in a jigsaw puzzle, a missing piece."*
Orson Wells, 1915-1985, from *Citizen Kane*

Jigsaw puzzles have been around almost as long as games. Early examples were handcrafted from wood. Lithograph pictures of country scenes, religious or moral subjects, geography, or historical figures were pasted on one or both sides of wooden puzzles. By the 1890s, jigsaw puzzles were considered great parlor entertainment, and many game manufacturers were producing them. Today, jigsaw puzzles remain a popular way to spend a rainy afternoon—and because of the variety, puzzles are also wonderful collectibles.

Jigsaw puzzles cover every subject you can think of. Humor, love, ethics, geography, history, as well as the past, present, and future, have all been depicted in jigsaw puzzle pictures. Often, the pictures on the front of the boxes are compelling enough to cause a collector to pick them up, but sometimes it's simply the topic that makes a jigsaw puzzle worth adding to a collection.

If you're interested in geography, then puzzles depicting maps or globes might be up your alley. Are you an outdoor enthusiast? Then puzzles with birds, bugs, mountains, lakes, or other natural wonders may have some appeal. How about puzzles with historical buildings or structures such as the White House in Washington, D.C., the Eiffel Tower in Paris, France, or the Great Pyramids in Egypt? If toys, balloons, and other playthings sound like more fun, then look for puzzles that feature these amusements. What about puzzles with a little more personality?

Puzzles featuring people from the pages of history, famous events, and television and movie personalities are highly collectible. Who wouldn't want to assemble George Washington crossing the Delaware, sort out Dick Tracy, piece together Frankenstein, or solve the mystery of the Hardy Boys' puzzle? How about helping the Bee Gees get it all together, putting Farrah Faucett's smile in place, or piecing together Captain Kangaroo? These puzzles are wonderful additions to any collection, but they only represent a fraction of the choices.

Specialty puzzles also attract a good deal of interest from collectors. Assemble the mystery puzzle and clues will appear "right before your very eyes." Go crazy trying to figure out which side is up on a two-sided puzzle. Look for the four different scenes revealed on a completed block puzzle—or marvel at the complexity of a three-dimensional jigsaw. Puzzle models of the White House, the Capitol, and other stately buildings are not only challenging to assemble, they are fun to collect. At least one company has developed a three-dimensional spherical jigsaw puzzle of the

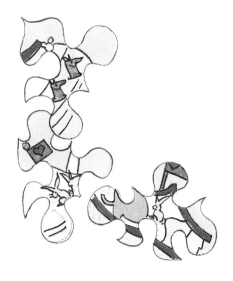

world. The amazing thing about this puzzle is that it's assembled without any interior support or glue. The interlocking pieces fit so tightly together that they stay in place during construction.

Jigsaw puzzles can be found at garage sales, thrift shops, church bazaars, and other secondhand sales; however, whenever you buy used puzzles there's a chance that some of the pieces will be missing. If you're spending a dollar or less, you might be willing to take the risk. Antique or wooden puzzles, on the other hand, might cost as much as $75. Most of us will probably rely on new puzzles to build our collections.

Retail prices range from a few dollars to around $50, depending on the size and type of puzzle. Department, toy, gift, and other stores carry jigsaw puzzles with 25 to 5,000 pieces. If you want to collect small puzzles at the best prices, check dollar and discount stores where they're sold for $1 or less.

Once your collection begins to grow, you'll have fun displaying it. Arrange puzzle boxes on shelves or on tables to be admired. Frame assembled puzzles between two pieces of Plexiglas to hang them on the wall, or place a completed puzzle on a table-top and cover it with glass. Three-dimensional puzzles can spruce up any room when displayed on table-tops or shelves.

Collecting jigsaw puzzles is fun and it can provide hours of relaxing entertainment as you piece together your finds. If you enjoy putting jigsaws together, then the idea of collecting them isn't so puzzling!

Related Collectibles: models, games, toys

46

Kaleidoscopes

···

*"There is no law of history any
more than of a kaleidoscope."*

John Ruskin, 1819-1900

The Scottish Physicist, Sir David Brewster, invented the kaleidoscope in 1815. "kaleidoscope" is a Greek word meaning "beautiful form to view," and that says it all. A veritable "rainbow" in a can, the kaleidoscope holds a whirling, twirling cavalcade of colors. Look through the hole at one end, hold the tube up to the light, spin the bottom of the kaleidoscope and watch beautiful geometric shapes flow in and out of sight. Stars, squares, circles, and an unlimited number of indescribable designs entertain the eye. The simplicity and the beauty of the kaleidoscope makes it a classic collectible that will never go out of style.

The kaleidoscope is an optical instrument which holds a series of reflecting mirrors. Bits of colorful glass, sand, shells, or other materials are sandwiched between two or more pieces of glass. As the bottom of the tube is turned, the material moves freely creating varied changes in form and design. The mirrors are used to create symmetrical shapes, and the results are amazing.

Although kaleidoscopes are not as common as they used to be, they are still available. Beautiful brass kaleidoscopes, dating fifty years or more, can be found in antique stores. The prices start at around one hundred dollars, and can go over $1,000. Kaleidoscopes rarely show up at flea markets, garage sales, or other low cost sales. For these reasons, you'll probably want to collect new kaleidoscopes.

New kaleidoscopes can be found in toy, nature, and science stores. The toy store variety tends to be made of stiff cardboard and have painted or embedded colorful designs which create geometric shapes when it's turned. Nature and science stores often carry brass or metal-cased kaleidoscopes. The highly

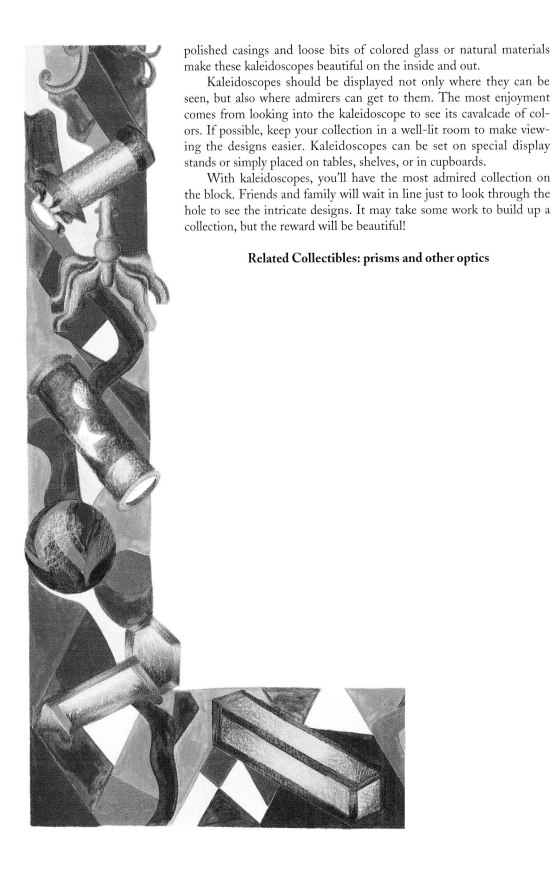

polished casings and loose bits of colored glass or natural materials make these kaleidoscopes beautiful on the inside and out.

Kaleidoscopes should be displayed not only where they can be seen, but also where admirers can get to them. The most enjoyment comes from looking into the kaleidoscope to see its cavalcade of colors. If possible, keep your collection in a well-lit room to make viewing the designs easier. Kaleidoscopes can be set on special display stands or simply placed on tables, shelves, or in cupboards.

With kaleidoscopes, you'll have the most admired collection on the block. Friends and family will wait in line just to look through the hole to see the intricate designs. It may take some work to build up a collection, but the reward will be beautiful!

Related Collectibles: prisms and other optics

47

Key Chains

···

"The used key is always bright."
Benjamin Franklin, 1706-1790

For anyone who has tried to carry a single key, the key chain has probably proved itself to be an invaluable invention. Like almost everything else, the key chain has gone from being a simple, practical device, to a highly personalized means of self expression. Today, there are almost as many different key chains as there are people using them. For this reason, key chains have become popular with collectors of all ages.

Key chains often reflect the personality and interests of the owner. Sports car enthusiasts may have a key chain with a Corvette, Ferrari, classic Mustang or other "hot" car parked at one end. Music buffs might carry a key chain with a musical note, staff, or even an instrument dangling opposite the keys. Cartoon characters, movie stars, sports, humor, and many other curiosities are well-represented on today's key chains, and probably the most popular type of key chains are souvenirs.

Key chains and travel just seem to go together. Have you gone to California, Oregon, Texas, Virginia, or New York lately? If so, you may have picked up one or more souvenir key chains for your collection. Many collectors specialize in key chains which bear the logo of a city, state, or country they've visited. The great thing about collecting souvenir key chains is that they're very easy to pack—just slip them into your pocket.

How about key chains from the tourist attractions your parents took you to on vacation? Crater Lake, Mount Rainier, Mammoth Caves, the Statue of Liberty, even the White House has been immortalized on key rings. Often these collectibles cost $5 or less, and typically, they are very easy to find.

How about taking the academic route? Key chains with college and university logos make wonderful collectibles. Look for key chains from the Big Twelve, PAC Ten, or the Ivy League. Select college key chains based on the school's mascot. The Oregon State Beavers, Texas A&M Aggies, and the Washington Huskies are but a few of the interesting mascots to choose from. Also, look for specialty key chains to help focus your collecting efforts.

Flashlights, pocketknives, whistles, and other special key chains offer the collector quite a bit of diversity. Even bottle openers, whistles, and small tools have been adapted for use on key chains. The options are seemingly endless—and that makes for great collecting.

Interesting key chains are a fairly recent invention, and they rarely show up at secondhand sales. For this reason, you should concentrate your collecting efforts at various retail stores. Discount, department, grocery, convenience, and specialty stores usually carry a wide assortment of key chains. Tourist attractions, visitor centers, and gift stores almost always have unique key chains for sale. Believe it or not, truck stops and automotive stores, too, offer a great variety as well.

As your key chain collection grows, you may want to display it. A piece of plywood, measuring about three feet square, will work well to display your collection. Ask one of your parents to help you pound small nails or hooks into the board, a few inches apart. Then, hang one key chain on each hook with the decorative side facing forward. The board can be leaned against or hung on the wall. As your collection grows, you can add more hooks and, if necessary, another board.

Collecting key chains is a fun way to express your interests—and, that might be the key to keeping you collecting for a long time!

Related Collectibles: keys, locks

48

Keys

....

"Tis in my memory lock'd,
And you yourself shall keep the key of it."
William Shakespeare, 1564-1616

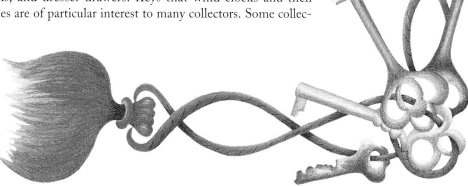

Since the days of the early Romans, keys have freed the mysteries hidden in locked boxes, behind doors, and secured by bars or fences. Diaries and other special books are sometimes under lock-and-key to hide their secrets from the casual reader. With a turn of a key, information, money, antiques, jewelry, and even people, have been granted protection and privacy. In our society, keys hold even greater prominence than safeguarding things.

We present our heroes with a "key to the city," even though it won't turn a single lock. The love of our lives holds the "key to our heart," even though a key hole can't be found. When we're perplexed, we look for the "key that will solve the puzzle." It's our high regard for them as a means to open possibilities, and the variety which makes keys a great collectible.

Over the past several centuries, many different kinds of keys have tumbled locks. Early keys were made of wood, iron, steel, and even gold. Today, light-weight metal is shaped into key blanks and then the keys are cut to match their locks. Perhaps the best way to begin collecting, is to decide what type of keys to collect.

For most collectors, older keys hold the greatest interest. Skeleton keys, dating back to the 1800s, are often forged in elegant and decorative style. These keys are examples of early craftsmanship and quality. Other collectible keys open padlocks, trunks, and dresser drawers. Keys that wind clocks and their chimes are of particular interest to many collectors. Some collectors look for tiny keys which once opened small boxes, book latches, and other little locks. If more modern keys are to your liking, then your options are even greater.

Keys that unlock suitcases, freezers, padlocks, and many other things are often stamped with the maker's name and logo. There are a large number of keys with the names and makes of automobiles stamped on them. Just make sure that you ask your parents before adding any household keys to your collection in case they are still needed.

If you can't find any keys at home to add to your collection, there are plenty of other places you can look. Some of the best places to begin your search for keys are antique shops, flea markets, and other secondhand sales. Also, a friendly locksmith might be a good source for adding new keys to your collection. The prices for keys can range from a few cents up to several dollars if they are sold without the matching lock. When a key is with its matching lock, the price can be as high as several hundred dollars.

Once you begin searching for keys, it may seem like they're everywhere. Remember—the key to being a successful collector is to keep your eyes open.

Related Collectibles: locks, key chains, books with keys and locks

49

Kitchen Collectibles

....

"Born in the garret, in the kitchen bred."
Lord Byron, 1788-1824

It's where we store our food, prepare the meals, and sometimes even eat. Enticing aromas permeate the air, beckoning us to gather in the kitchen. The smell of coffee brewing, cookies baking, or breakfast sizzling on the griddle, wouldn't happen without the help of a few special tools, though. Over time, these tools have become quite specialized and very collectible.

Since about 1850, mass-produced kitchen gadgets have been invented, patented, and sold at an astonishing rate. Everything from apple peelers to waffle irons have been placed in the hands of the home chef to make cooking easier, faster, and better. Competition for consumer dollars lead to rapid innovation with hundreds of different models of mashers, shakers, scoops, and other basic culinary equipment. For the collector, this means that there are an unlimited number of kitchen collectibles to search for.

At the turn of the century, every kitchen was equipped for pitting, chopping, mixing, grating, peeling, and preparing fresh foods. There were very few processed foods, so the well-prepared cook had to stock almost as many tools as the local mechanic. Among the more prominent kitchen collectibles are rolling pins, choppers, can openers, and spatulas—but the most unbeatable kitchen collectible has to be the eggbeater.

Since 1856, there have been over 1,000 patents issued for eggbeaters. With every inventor believing that he could "build a better beater," collectors can find a wide assortment of sizes and designs. Hundreds of rotary crank, turbine, squeeze power, and other styles have been documented, with new ones turning up each year. In fact, eggbeaters are so unique, many collectors specialize in them. Over the years, everything from plastic to metal has been used to make eggbeaters. Among the most popular are the all-metal models which often date from the 1930s or earlier. If you're having mixed feelings about collecting eggbeaters, then consider some other kitchen collectible.

Wooden spoons, pie edgers, ladles, bottle openers, potato mashers, or just about any other preparation tool can enhance a kitchen collection. Stew pots, mixing bowls, frying pans, measuring cups, cookie cutters,

and other kitchenware are also fair game. You can specialize in a particular type of collectible such as egg cups, assemble a collection which represents your favorite area of cooking—baking, for example, or collect everything and anything you like!

Most collectors look for kitchen collectibles that date from the 1940s or later. Kitchenware from this era tends to be made of either all metal or wood and metal. This isn't a sure-fire way to tell how old a piece is, but it's a good rule-of-thumb. The best way to learn about kitchen collectibles is to purchase a good price guide and study it. Once you know what to look for, the trick becomes finding it.

Garage sales are probably the best place to find affordable kitchen collectibles. Even though you might have to look pretty hard, the prices of garage sale kitchenware are usually $5 or less. Flea market, antique store, and even auction store prices have risen steadily, putting some of the finest kitchen collectibles out of reach for young collectors. Some eggbeaters, for example, can cost as much as $1,000 or more. Granted, most of them are in the $20 to $40 range, but even at those prices, it can take a while to save up for just one. Be prepared, then, to wear out some shoe leather to build your collection.

Displaying your kitchen collection is half of the fun. Many items can be arranged on shelves, tables, or in cupboards. Some kitchenware can be hung by hooks on the wall. Use your imagination and incorporate fruit labels, packaging, or anything else that may enhance your display.

Collecting kitchenware is fun, and, before you know it, things will really get cooking!

Related Collectibles: napkin rings, candlesticks, or other meal-related collectibles

50

Lanterns and Flashlights

"But up in his room by artificial light
My father paints the summer."
Richard Purdy Wilbur, 1921-

Ever since early man built the first campfire, we have enjoyed the freedom provided by artificial light. Reading, writing, playing games and other recreational pursuits would only be daytime events if it weren't for our ability to have light on demand. The portrait of American business might be different today if entrepreneurs weren't able to "burn the midnight oil," while tending to business. It is, perhaps, our reliance on artificial light which has made collecting lanterns and flashlights such a popular pastime.

Lanterns, unlike lamps, were designed to be carried from one place to another. The broad base for stability, spill-proof fuel reservoir, wire protected glass globe, and a handle located well away from the flame, made the lantern a very useful tool. Long before the flashlight was invented, policemen carried lanterns while making their rounds in the dark of night. Firemen, construction workers, and many other professionals relied on the glow of kerosene and other fuels to light their way—but it was the railroad men from America's past who come to mind most often when the word lantern is mentioned.

Railroad conductors checking tickets carried lanterns as they passed through the train at night. Brakemen, who maintained the train's brakes and couplings, relied on lanterns to make evening repairs and investigate crashes, fires, or yard accidents. Railroad lanterns were also an important means of communication. The light from the lantern could be used to signal or flag down approaching trains. Today, railroad lanterns are prized by those who collect them.

Virtually all railroad lanterns are marked with the name or initials of the railroad line they were used on. The Baltimore & Ohio, Great Northern, and Leigh Valley are just a few of the names that you might find engraved on a lantern's metal base. Established collectors look for highly polished brass, decorated metal work, and elegant globes. These early, decorative lanterns can be both difficult to find and expensive; however, many recent lanterns do fall into the "affordable" category.

Simple, metal lanterns can often be purchased at flea markets for $15 or less. Occasionally, they can be found at farm auctions. Before you begin your collection, you must first know what to look for. Try to find lanterns that are complete and in good condition. Often, old lanterns will be thick with dirt and mud from many years of hard use, but don't let that bother you. Ask a parent or adult friend to help you clean it up.

First, empty any of the leftover fuel into a tin can. Gas, kerosene, and other lantern fuel is both toxic and flammable, so let an adult dispose of it properly. Then, carefully take the lantern apart and clean each piece with a damp cloth. The globe can be washed in soapy water—but be careful. Wet glass is slippery and easy to drop. Once the lantern is thoroughly dry, it can be put back together. Remember—you should never light an old lantern. Excessive dirt or broken pieces makes lighting fuel-burning lanterns very dangerous. So, if you want to use your lanterns, consider battery operated lights.

After 1940, battery operated railroad lanterns came in to use, and since these are not usually marked with the railroad line, they are not in great demand. Keep your eyes open for these affordable lamps for your collection. Also, look for skating, driving, and utility lanterns which can be either kerosene or battery operated. If you live in an area where it's difficult to find affordable lanterns, perhaps you should consider collecting modern flashlights.

Flashlights first came into use around 1900, some 30 years after the widespread use of batteries. With so many different companies making flashlights over the years, the sizes and styles are unlimited.

Plastic and metal, plain or fancy, flashlights are everywhere. Collect the itty-bitty promotional lights attached to key chains, the great big industrial sized lamps, or any flashlight that appeals to you. Flashlights can be found at discount, automotive, department, grocery, and many other retail stores. Occasionally, too, they even show up at church bazaars and other secondhand sales. Most flashlights are priced at $10 or less—and displaying your light collection couldn't be easier.

Lanterns and flashlights are perfect for shelf displays. They rest nicely on their base or lens down. Key chain flashlights can be hung on the wall or on special display boards. Take a piece of plywood and pound small nails in straight, evenly spaced rows. Then, hang the key chain flashlights on the nails to display. The board can either be hung or leaned up against the wall.

Collecting lanterns and flashlights can be a lot of fun and, they'll never leave you in the dark!

Related Collectibles: candles, small lamps

51

Locks

....

"A zealous locksmith died of late,
And did arrive at heaven gate,
He stood without and would not knock,
Because he meant to pick the lock."

Anonymous

The oldest lock in recorded history was found in the ruins of the Palace of Khorsabad, near ancient Nineveh. This lock, which dates back to 2000 B.C., was opened with a long wooden bolt. The bolt has a pattern of pegs which corresponds to the pegs in the lock. When the pegs were matched up, the lock opened. Although simple in design, this was the forerunner of the locks that we use today.

Later developments in lock technology gave us ward, tumbler, and combination locks—but the way locks work isn't the only thing that makes them unique.

The shape, any stamped names or decorations, and what the lock is made of, determines how appealing it will be to collectors. Locks come in a variety of shapes. Canteen, pancake, square, and heart-shaped locks are among the most common. The locks with the greatest appeal tend to be those with decorative pictures or logos on them. Many of the early nineteenth century locks are striking examples of decorative iron work with eagles, swords, crosses, shields or logos cast into the front plate. Brass and bronze are far more popular than iron or steel locks. Although these beautifully crafted locks are very attractive, they're also quite expensive, costing one hundred dollars or more. For this reason, most young collectors look for steel locks.

Finding old locks is easier than one might think. The first place to check is in your own home. Ask your parents if they have any old locks they don't need anymore. Most families have a drawer with old keys and locks stashed away for future use. Sometimes the drawer contains some real treasures! Also, check with friends and grandparents to see if they have any old locks to help you get started.

Once you have exhausted your personal resources, it's time to look elsewhere. Garage sales, flea markets, and auctions are great hunting grounds for the lock collector, and the prices are usually quite reasonable. Other possibilities include befriending professionals who might find old locks in the course of their

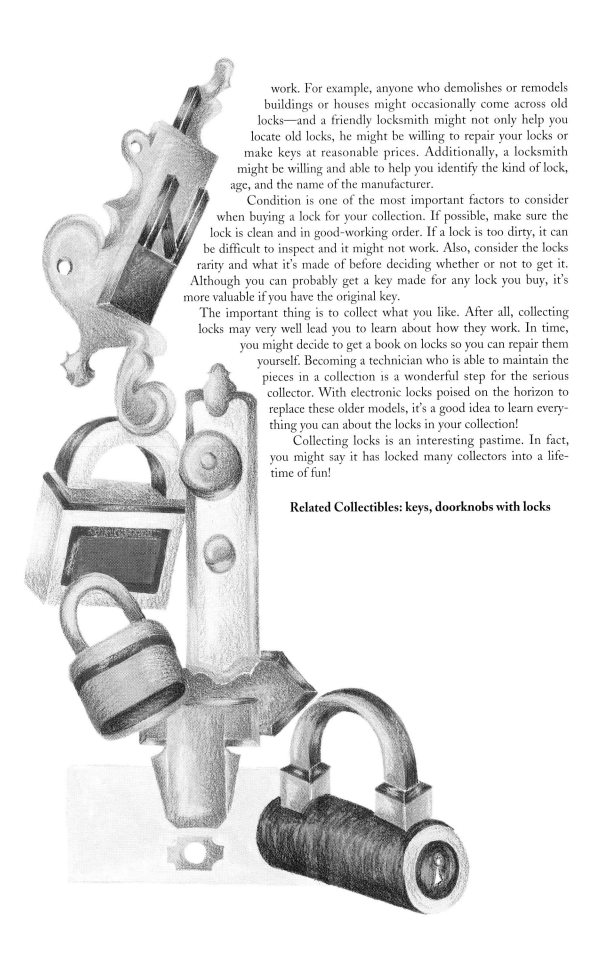

work. For example, anyone who demolishes or remodels buildings or houses might occasionally come across old locks—and a friendly locksmith might not only help you locate old locks, he might be willing to repair your locks or make keys at reasonable prices. Additionally, a locksmith might be willing and able to help you identify the kind of lock, age, and the name of the manufacturer.

Condition is one of the most important factors to consider when buying a lock for your collection. If possible, make sure the lock is clean and in good-working order. If a lock is too dirty, it can be difficult to inspect and it might not work. Also, consider the locks rarity and what it's made of before deciding whether or not to get it. Although you can probably get a key made for any lock you buy, it's more valuable if you have the original key.

The important thing is to collect what you like. After all, collecting locks may very well lead you to learn about how they work. In time, you might decide to get a book on locks so you can repair them yourself. Becoming a technician who is able to maintain the pieces in a collection is a wonderful step for the serious collector. With electronic locks poised on the horizon to replace these older models, it's a good idea to learn everything you can about the locks in your collection!

Collecting locks is an interesting pastime. In fact, you might say it has locked many collectors into a lifetime of fun!

Related Collectibles: keys, doorknobs with locks

52

LUNCH BOXES

········

"There's no such thing as a free lunch."
Milton Friedman, 1912-

Peanut butter and jelly sandwiches were once carried around in recycled, square metal pails. These pails, complete with handles, originally contained crackers, bread, and other products, and were designed to be used as lunch boxes once the products were used up. The popularity of these early pails lead to the manufacturing of lunch boxes. By 1930, colorful, lithographed lunch boxes, that were designed to appeal to children, were being mass-produced. Lunch box manufacturers such as Aladdin Industries, American Thermos, Decoware, and Ohio Art created an area of collecting that's almost as popular as it is fun!

Although the earliest lunch boxes are of interest to many advertising and box collectors, character pails are in the most demand. In 1950, Aladdin Industries produced what may be the first real character lunch box. A steel Hopalong Cassidy lunch box with decal decorations was released to a hungry young crowd. This Western hero not only caught the bad guys, but he also protected the bologna sandwiches eaten by America's youth. A few years later, American Thermos released the first fully lithographed steel lunch box with a matching thermos. With this 1953 Roy Rogers box, lunch-time fun was just beginning.

Lunch boxes have been made of steel, vinyl, and plastic. The steel pails often have colorful lithographic pictures on them, making them very appealing to collectors. In the 1980s, when the cost of metal pails skyrocketed, a new interest in vinyl and plastic boxes was born.

There are well over 500 different lunch boxes covering a variety of subjects, personalities, and television shows. Like most collectibles, the most popular topics are the most familiar. Western themes such as "The Rifleman," "Gunsmoke," "Bonanza," and other cowboys ride high in the saddle. Cartoon characters including the Flintstones, Peanuts, and the Berenstain Bears have lunched with collectors for years. If you like action figures, Batman, Robin Hood, Superman and the rest of the Super Friends could be the heroes of your collection. Barbie, Dr. Seuss, the Muppets, and other favorites have also been featured on lunch buckets—and sports teams, toys and movies have also joined us

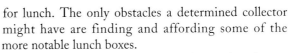

for lunch. The only obstacles a determined collector might have are finding and affording some of the more notable lunch boxes.

Many lunch boxes, especially the steel pails, can be quite expensive. Prices in excess of $100 are not uncommon; however, if you look hard and get lucky, you can still find some great buys at garage sales, auctions, flea markets and other secondhand sales. Like so many areas of collecting, it's important to get a good reference guide so you can familiarize yourself with current values. The value of a lunch box depends on a few simple things.

The material the box is made of is critical to its value. Steel pails are generally more valuable since they are older than vinyl or plastic. The condition of a lunch box is also important. Dents, scratches, or writing will lower the value. Most lunch pails originally came with a matching thermos—which, if found with the box, is quite desirable. Finally, the subject on the front of the box and how scarce it is, will also determine its value. While collecting lunch boxes can be an expensive hobby, it doesn't have to be.

New, plastic lunch boxes with decals and stickers can be purchased at retail stores for less than $5. While these pails may not be as appealing as some of the older models, they should be within the budgets of most young collectors. Look for subjects that interest you, and don't be afraid to actually use your lunch box collection. Some collectors might speculate that even today's lunch pails will someday be valuable, but because of mass-production, it probably won't happen in our lifetime. Besides, collecting should be fun—so, for a collectible that covers a wide range of topics, let's do lunch—lunch boxes that is!

Related Collectibles: thermoses, lithographed tins and canisters

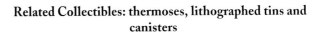

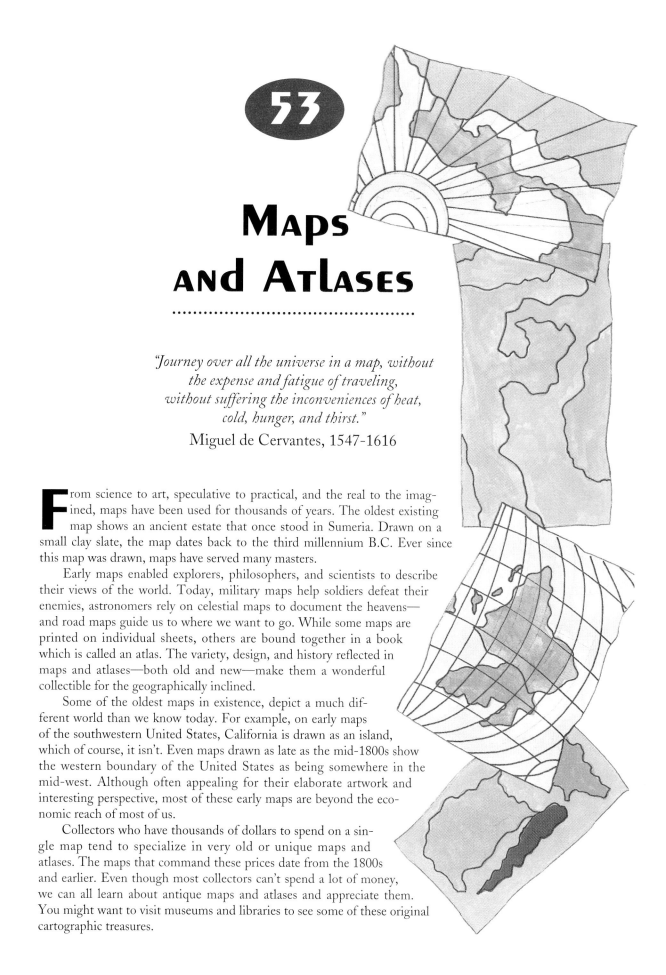

53

Maps
and Atlases

···

*"Journey over all the universe in a map, without
the expense and fatigue of traveling,
without suffering the inconveniences of heat,
cold, hunger, and thirst."*

Miguel de Cervantes, 1547-1616

From science to art, speculative to practical, and the real to the imagined, maps have been used for thousands of years. The oldest existing map shows an ancient estate that once stood in Sumeria. Drawn on a small clay slate, the map dates back to the third millennium B.C. Ever since this map was drawn, maps have served many masters.

Early maps enabled explorers, philosophers, and scientists to describe their views of the world. Today, military maps help soldiers defeat their enemies, astronomers rely on celestial maps to document the heavens—and road maps guide us to where we want to go. While some maps are printed on individual sheets, others are bound together in a book which is called an atlas. The variety, design, and history reflected in maps and atlases—both old and new—make them a wonderful collectible for the geographically inclined.

Some of the oldest maps in existence, depict a much different world than we know today. For example, on early maps of the southwestern United States, California is drawn as an island, which of course, it isn't. Even maps drawn as late as the mid-1800s show the western boundary of the United States as being somewhere in the mid-west. Although often appealing for their elaborate artwork and interesting perspective, most of these early maps are beyond the economic reach of most of us.

Collectors who have thousands of dollars to spend on a single map tend to specialize in very old or unique maps and atlases. The maps that command these prices date from the 1800s and earlier. Even though most collectors can't spend a lot of money, we can all learn about antique maps and atlases and appreciate them. You might want to visit museums and libraries to see some of these original cartographic treasures.

Choosing an area to specialize in isn't easy for map collectors. Maps are fascinating and they appeal to almost anyone who is interested in geography. There are wetlands, railroad, real estate, census, fire insurance and many other special-use maps to consider; however, not all of these maps are readily available to collectors.

One special map that is easy to find is the road map. Road maps showing the major cities, highways, and points of interest in a particular state are sometimes available at no cost. State tourist offices should have a toll-free telephone number that you can call to request a free road map. Be sure to confirm the cost, if any, before asking them to send you a map. If you travel by car, stop at tourist information booths to pick up free maps—or look at map and book stores for commercially printed road maps that cost $5 or less.

Another type of map you might want to collect is the topographic map. Topographic maps show hills, valleys, rivers, lakes, cities, and other special features of the land. Topographic maps cover the entire United States in one of several different series. Maps from the 7.5- and 15-minute series are still available, but the 30- and 60-minute series have been out of print for awhile. Sometimes old topographic maps show up at auctions, garage sales, or at book and paper shows. Naturally, if you find a map that you like, go ahead and add it to your collection; however, the best way to build a topographic map collection is to purchase new maps that are still in print.

Collecting new topographic maps allows you to plan your collection. Do you want to collect maps of a particular city, county, or state? Do you want to specialize in the 7.5- or 15-minute series? Answer these questions and you're almost ready to start collecting.

Before you can actually buy the map that you want, you have to understand how to find it. Each map sheet, regardless of which series it's from, is called a quadrangle. These quadrangles are named after a city, town, or other prominent feature which can be found on that map. Each sheet also has a unique reference code which identifies it. Using the name and reference code, you can track down a specific quadrangle.

New topographic maps can sometimes be purchased locally at map, book, or outdoor stores—but the greatest selection of topographic maps is available from the United States Geological Survey (USGS) in Virginia.

There are two ways to find out the names and reference codes of specific quadrangles. First, you can go to the library and ask if they have the *Index to Topographic and Other Map Coverage* for your state. If they do, look up the quadrangles and then place an order with the USGS at (703) 648-6892. Topographic maps from the USGS are priced at less than $5. When you call the USGS, be sure to ask the customer representative to send you information on some of the other maps they have for sale.

Once you begin learning about different maps, there's no telling what you might collect. In fact, you might even decide to collect atlases.

World atlases, particularly those from 1900 and later, can be found reasonably priced at garage sales, used book stores, flea markets, and other secondhand sales. It's interesting to look at which country names and boundaries have changed since the atlas was printed. Specialty atlases such as county, school, and railroad often include historical essays as well as maps.

Maps don't just take us from "here to there." They're a great way to learn about geography, history, and the world that we live in. In fact, maps might just put you on the road to building a great cartographic collection.

Related Collectibles: world globes, books on cartography

Marbles

"The little toy dog is covered with dust,
But sturdy and staunch he stands;
And the little toy soldier is red with rust,
And his musket molds in his hands;
Time was when the little toy dog was new,
And the soldier was passing fair;
And that was the time when our Little Boy Blue
Kissed them and put them there."

Eugene Field, 1850-1895

The Little Boy Blue that Eugene Field was talking about in the above quote probably had a slew of marbles stashed in his pocket, too! From the mid-1800s until the dawn of electronic games, marbles were a familiar amusement. Schoolyard games of chance and skill were played with the best shooters taking all of the marbles. There were even state and national marble championships until the 1940s. While kids still play with them today, early marbles have become popular with collectors.

Old marbles made of clay, stone, pottery and glass have been discovered through-out the world. Ancient marbles have been uncovered at Colonial Williamsburg, Pompeii, and in King Tut's tomb. Just how long marbles have been around is uncertain, but 4,000 years or more seems likely.

Most antique glass marbles were made in Germany between 1850 and 1915. Craftsmen shaped their molten marbles into won-derful master-pieces that are as unique as the artists themselves. In fact, antique marbles are like snowflakes, no two are exactly alike. Handmade marbles are very beautiful, but prices ranging from $100 or more, put them well beyond the reach of most young collectors. Fortunately, there is a more affordable alternative.

By 1915, machine-made marbles had replaced handcrafted spheres, and they were rolling into school yards by the droves. Today, mass-produced marbles from the 1950s and 1960s can be picked up at flea markets, antique stores, and other secondhand sales for a few dollars. At prices like this, you can afford to buy what you like and not worry about the actual value; however, before you spend any serious money on marbles, you should become familiar with the types and values.

A good price guide, a knowledgeable collector, and a trusted dealer are essential resources for beginning marble collectors. Many reproduction marbles are on the market today, and dealers sometimes knowingly charge much more than a marble is worth. Even seasoned marble collectors fall prey to these shady deals—so do your homework, seek the advice of others, and, hopefully, no one will take advantage of you.

As your collection grows, you will want to find interesting ways to display your marbles. Try to attend a marble show to see how dealers display them. Wooden blocks with circular depressions, custom racks, and other specialty display items should be for sale; however, for a low cost display option, place your marbles on a colorful towel or a strip of thick terry cloth. With a towel or a piece of terry cloth underneath, your marbles should stay in place on a flat shelf or table.

Collecting marbles is fun—so get out there and start looking—and remember: Marble collectors play for keeps!

Related Collectibles: marble games

Matchbook Covers

*"You are a king by your own fireside, as much
as any monarch in his throne."*
Miguel de Cervantes, 1547-1616

In 1855, John Walker, an English chemist, was stirring a mixture of potash and antimony in the hopes of making a combustible which could fire a gun. When the mixture stuck to the end of his wooden stir stick, he began to wipe it off on the stone beneath his feet. The scraping caused the mixture burst into flames, sparking the invention of safety matches. Walker's mishap had another result: The discovery of matchbook covers as a hot collectible.

Matchbook covers is another great collectible that requires only a little pocket change and persistence. Look around—matchbooks are everywhere. They are sometimes colorful reminders of the places we've gone, the people we've met, or the things we've done. Special events are often commemorated with one or more matchbook designs. Businesses, politicians, and places have all appeared on matchbook covers—that's why so many people, even "non-collectors," have lots of matchbooks lying around.

Some collectors start by picking up every matchbook they see. While there may be great satisfaction in building a collection so quickly, it may not be the most rewarding way. Thousands of matchbook covers might be impressive, but it's difficult to care for and display this volume. Instead, consider focusing on one of over 100 different matchbook cover categories.

For example, some collectors look for commemorative matchbook covers marking the World's Fair, the Apollo space flights, major sporting, or other notable events. Others collect matchbook covers from restaurants, hotels, gas stations, or other businesses. Matchbook covers with jokes, cartoons, product advertising, or private addresses printed on them are also quite collectible. You just have to know where to find them.

Old matchbook covers can sometimes be found at flea markets and antique stores for $1 or less. These can be particularly fun additions to your collection, but if you want your collection to grow, look for matchbook covers wherever you go.

Be selective about what you collect. Collect only covers that are in new or mint condition. Make sure that the strike plate hasn't been used and that the cover itself isn't ripped or discolored. When you handle matchbook covers, remember that safety comes first.

117

Matches are flammable, and they can catch fire without warning; therefore, with the help of your parents or another adult, remove the staple and the matches with a pocket or kitchen knife. Once the matches have been removed, either give them to the adult for future use, or soak them in water for a few minutes and then throw them away. After all your covers are empty, you are ready to display your collection.

Matchbook covers can be displayed in many different ways. One of the best ways is to place them neatly into a photograph album. This allows you to easily flip through the pages to view your collection; however, if there are some special covers you'd like to see more often, then you can display them on the wall.

There are store-bought wall racks specially made for displaying matchbook covers. These racks hold 50 or more covers and they make colorful wall decorations. Another way to show off your collection is to keep them in a large glass bowl or jar. Although it's difficult to read individual covers, it will give a sense of the collection as a whole. Finally, some collectors place their covers on an old table-top and then brush shellac over them. This approach is rather permanent, but it can be very attractive.

Collecting matchbook covers is a fun way to keep track of where you've been, what you've seen, and who you've met. Matchbook covers are easy to find, affordable, and easily displayed. In short, matchbook covers are one hot collectible that won't leave you out in the cold!

Related Collectibles: match holders, match safes

56

Military Collectibles

"I still remember the refrain of one of the most popular barracks ballads of that day, which proclaimed most proudly that old soldiers never die; they just fade away. I now close my military career and just fade away."
General Douglas MacArthur, 1880-1964

The role that the military has played in the history of man is enormous. The protection of our borders, the defense of weaker countries, and the preservation of national pride, are among the proudest achievements of our nation's service men and women. Everyone from enlisted soldiers to generals, has in some way contributed to the military's prestige. It is the legacy of these individuals which has encouraged so many to collect military items.

The variety of military collectibles is almost endless. That's why most collectors specialize in either a particular item such as belt buckles, or in a specific era such as World War II. Even if you specialize, there will be a great variety of items to choose from.

Canteens, helmets, uniforms, insignias, mess kits, and other government-issued items are widely collected. The prices can range from a few dollars for a recent canteen, to several thousands of dollars for a Civil War Surgeon's kit. Naturally, the age, scarcity, and condition of a piece plays a major role in determining its value. Don't let a few high prices keep you away, though. There are many affordable military collectibles. Among the most reasonably priced are recent patches.

Each branch, company, and unit of the service has a number of unique patches that are worn on uniforms. Eagles, flags, special unit emblems, and other designs offer great variety. These patches are usually priced at $5 or less, and can be found at any surplus store. Other affordable military collectibles include caps, belts, and hats, which can often be found at prices of $10 or less; however, if price is no object, then consider one of the most prestigious military collectibles—medals.

Military medals that were awarded for bravery are very scarce and highly sought after by collectors. Often, these medals are kept in the family and passed down from one generation to the next. That's why these rare medals are priced so high when they're offered for sale.

Another type of medal which can be found more easily are those given to soldiers for fighting in a particular battle. These medals were not as highly regarded as those awarded for bravery, and were sometimes given away, sold, or discarded. Even though there were more examples of these group medals, certain ones are quite rare and can command high prices. If you decide to collect medals, you will need to do some homework.

Many medals are being reproduced and sold as genuine. This could mean that the $25 medal that you bought, is only worth $2. In order to avoid unknowingly buying reproductions, become familiar with as many medals and prices as you can. Price guides, reputable dealers, and other collectors are all excellent ways to learn about your hobby. If you're able to find original medals that are affordable, they're sure to become the centerpieces of your collection.

Another great military collectible is the photograph. Chances are that your family and friends have a few pictures of soldiers that you could make a copy of for your collection. Another reason to consider collecting photographs of soldiers is that they're among the most affordable military collectibles.

As with most collections, much of the enjoyment comes from meeting others who share similar interests. Drop in at the local surplus store, attend military collectibles shows, and if you're in an area where they have them, go to civil war reenactments. Take the time to talk with collectors and dealers while you search for new items to add to your collection. Along the way, pick up a good price guide to help you avoid making costly mistakes.

Military collectibles are a time-honored tradition—and it's a hobby that can't be beat!

Related Collectibles: non-military medals, badges, and patches

57

Movies

....

*"The fact is, I am quite happy in a movie,
even a bad movie. Other people, so I have read,
treasure memorable moments in their lives."*
Walker Percy, 1916-1990

Who wouldn't want to spend the afternoon with their favorite movie star? Wouldn't it be great if Jim Carry, the Olson Twins, or all 101 Dalmatians could hang out at your house and eat popcorn? Well, through the miracle of modern technology, they all can. It happens through the magic of the big screen as seen through your television. Movie stores and video departments in book, grocery, and convenience stores, have made movies one of the most accessible collectibles of the 1990s.

In fact, many people collect movies and don't even know they do. More than 75% of us own videocassette recorders and we rent or buy more than four billion videos each year. Go look on the shelf or in the drawer where your family keeps the videos. If your family is like most, you probably have a wide variety of movies in-house already. Drama, comedy, adventure, animation, science fiction—we seem to love it all—and, why not? Besides their great entertainment value, movies give us a reason to relax and enjoy each other's company. So, if you like big stars, great stories, and have a VCR, then collecting movies might be a blockbuster of an idea.

Collectors who are actively building their library specialize in a specific type of film, star, or subject matter. For example, some movie buffs collect only science fiction films. Others look for films featuring Tom Cruise, John Wayne, or another one of their favorite stars. They try to collect every movie that this person has ever made. Some collectors might assemble a library featuring only films with animals as a major part of the story line. If you think about it, the options for a movie collection are almost endless.

Used videos are sold at garage sales, flea markets, thrift stores, and other secondhand sales. Sometimes this is the only way to get old, out-of-print videos. Although the prices of used movies are generally better than new videos, be careful. Warping of the cartridge, tears in the tape, or weakness from over-use can go undetected with only a visual inspection. Whenever possible, play all used videos to make sure they work before you buy them. Naturally, you can also build your movie collection with new videos.

Buying new movies is the safest alternative, and it insures that your videos will hold up for awhile. The prices

for new movies generally range from $7 for older releases, to about $30 for the new films. With the availability of videos today, collecting movies has never been easier.

Many movie collectors are following the path of their childhood, collecting Disney and other animated films they have watched growing up. This is a great way to preserve and share memories over the years. It can turn an average evening with friends, into a party.

While movie collections are rarely displayed, it's important to store them properly. Keep videos stored away from direct sunlight in a cool, dust free environment. It's important to follow the manufacturer's directions for cleaning your VCR. If you don't, then you might damage your tapes. Finally, try to view each of your videos periodically. If you don't watch and enjoy the movies in your collection, then you might lose interest.

Collecting movies is fun, and it might just be your ticket to a great collection.

Related Collectibles: movie posters, soundtracks, and movie memorabilia

58

MUSIC BOXES

·······································

"Musick is the thing of the world that I love most."
Samuel Pepys, 1633-1703

The cylinder slowly turns as the music flows from the porcelain box. A metal comb is pulled across teeth that are tuned to specific pitches. A tiny dancer twirls as "ting, tong, ting," a metallic melody, is heard. Music boxes have long been the favorites of young and old alike. Their unique design, intricate craftsmanship, and beauty has enticed many generations of collectors to fill their shelves with these mechanical wonders.

The Swiss watchmaker, Antoine Favre invented the music box in 1796. Originally, single-song music boxes were placed in watches, snuff boxes, and later, in a variety of ornamental objects. By the 1820s, music boxes were being mass-produced—and in the mid-nineteenth century, the mechanical instruments began playing more than one tune. These early disk and cylinder models were the CD players of their time. Families gathered in the parlor, cranked the music box, and listened to its beautiful melodies.

Improvements and new inventions in mechanically produced sound changed the way people listened to music, and by 1914, music boxes had been replaced by the phonograph. The role of the music box changed from a central form of entertainment for adults, to only an occasional amusement, but small, figural music boxes continued to delight children, so production continued.

Today, renewed interest in early music boxes has created a demand for new and more intricate examples. Collector's clubs, newsletters, and specialty stores support the interests of those who can't resist these enchanting boxes. The variety of designs, styles, and music featured in these boxes has created a big challenge for collectors. In fact, it would be impossible to collect one of every music box ever made. For that reason, most collectors specialize in particular types or categories of music boxes.

There are two different types of music boxes. There are still music boxes (which have no visible moving parts) and animated music boxes (in which one or more figures on the box are in motion as the music plays). Both types of music boxes have strong collecting appeal.

Still music boxes are probably the easiest to find, and they're the most affordable with prices beginning at just a few dollars. Simple in design, still music boxes are often topped with one or more figurines that are fashioned to suit the music. For example, a music box which plays the song "Take Me Out to the Ball Game," might feature a little boy standing at home plate holding a bat and ball. While most collections include several still music boxes, there may only be a few animated examples.

Animated music boxes have figures which nod, twirl, glide from side to side, bounce up and down, or move in some other way. A mouse might run up the clock, a ballerina may twirl, or the wheels on a train might spin around. There's no telling what action will occur when you wind an animated music box. The delicate nature of the works, and the sophistication of the movements is the primary reason that animated music boxes are so expensive. They are precision instruments with prices ranging from $25 to over $1,000. If your collection includes both still and animated music boxes, you may want to specialize in a particular category.

There are many different categories for music box collectors to choose from. There are music boxes with clowns, animals, musical instruments, cartoon characters, trains, cars, and more. Some music boxes feature doctors, nurses, teachers, musicians and other recognizable professions. The holidays, too, are common music box themes. Although there are music boxes for Halloween, Mother's Day, Easter, and others, the most popular are probably those that celebrate Christmas. Nativity scenes, Santa, snowmen, toy soldiers, nutcrackers, and other Christmas-time sights are often featured in music boxes as a favorite carol plays. In addition to the types and categories of music boxes, there are a few special features you might want to look for.

Some music boxes have a light which comes on when the key is wound. Lighted music boxes are especially nice to have in your room at night while you go to sleep. Musical snow globes and Christmas ornaments are also special, and you might want to collect a few of these as well.

Music boxes are a wonderful collectible which can encompass a variety of interests. If you enjoy music, then collecting these treasures might keep you humming all day!

Related Collectibles: musical watches, instruments

124

MUSICAL INSTRUMENTS

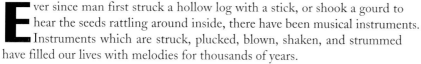

"The isle is full of noises,
Sounds and sweet airs, that give delight, and hurt not.
Sometimes a thousand twangling instruments
Will hum about mine ears; and sometimes voices,
That, if I then had wak'd after long sleep,
Will make me sleep again."

William Shakespeare, 1564-1616

Ever since man first struck a hollow log with a stick, or shook a gourd to hear the seeds rattling around inside, there have been musical instruments. Instruments which are struck, plucked, blown, shaken, and strummed have filled our lives with melodies for thousands of years.

It would be difficult to go anywhere in civilization without hearing some kind of music. We hear it in the car, elevator, doctor's office, grocery store, and in just about every other public place—and even though many people may be hearing the same piece of music, the personal nature of the words and melody makes it special to each of us. It's both the connection we have with the music and the craftsmanship of the instruments that make them popular with collectors.

Most collectors specialize in the type of instruments they play. For example, guitar players might have over a dozen guitars in their collections, and they might play every one of them. Depending upon the style, age, size, and the material that each guitar was made from, they probably all have very different sounds. Instruments can be collected not only for how they look, but how they sound.

If you don't play an instrument, but would still like to collect them, there are several that you could "play at" while collecting. Twelve of the most friendly for the musically challenged are bongo drums, bugles, castanets, cymbals, harmonicas, jingle clogs, moraccos,

recorders, tambourines, triangles, wrist bells, and xylophones. Practice any of these as much or as little as you like to produce rhythms or simple chords. On the lighter side, you might want to add kazoos, mouth harps, minstrel bones, and musical saws to your unique assembly of instruments.

If you decide to collect instruments but have no intention of ever playing them, then you might consider specializing in foreign, handmade, or antique instruments. These are often fine examples of craftsmanship which can be admired for their beauty as well as their sound.

Musical instruments can be purchased new or used. If you don't know what to look for in a good playing instrument, you might want to buy only new instruments. If on the other hand, you are knowledgeable enough to buy serious instruments that are used, or if you are collecting instruments mostly to look at, then you can consider buying them secondhand.

Many music stores sell used instruments; however, there are several other places you can look. Church bazaars, flea markets, garage sales, and auctions frequently include musical instruments in their sales. But don't limit the search to these general sales. Check the local newspaper which probably has a classified section just for instruments. Also, the local pawn shop might be a good place to look. Many quality instruments are left at pawn shops and then later sold at discount prices. Keep in mind that no matter what type of instrument you're looking for, condition is everything. An instrument from an unknown maker could be twice as valuable as one made by a famous company, just because of its condition. Don't buy any instrument that isn't in good playing order.

Collecting instruments is a fun way to expand your interest in music. It's almost certain that with a musical instrument collection, you'll never have to depend on the radio for tunes or background noise again.

Related Collectibles: sheet music, music boxes

60

Napkin Rings

·······················

*"We were to do more business after dinner; but
after dinner is after dinner - an old saying and a true . . ."*
Jonathan Swift, 1667-1745

Napkin rings became popular tableware in the late 1800s. During that time, napkins were made of cloth (instead of paper which is often used today). With early table linens getting a good washing only once a week, unique napkin rings helped to identify which napkin belonged to whom. And, often, the napkin rings reflected the interests, professions, or hobbies of the person using it. For this reason, napkin rings were made in a wide variety of styles which included a mind-boggling array of subjects. It's the variety and elegance of these old rings which has piqued interest in them as collectibles.

Certainly, the Victorian silver-plated figural napkin rings are among the most desirable. Delicate designs, amazing detail, and artistic excellence make these antiques highly sought after. Nature, story book characters, cupids, and other topics are common subjects for napkin rings. These beautiful relics of a more gentile time command high prices, so if you want to collect figural napkin rings, you might want to look for newer ones. Today, there are many reproduction figural napkin rings on the market. These higher-end new rings, can sometimes be found in department stores for $20 or less.

Napkin rings made of glass, wood, wicker, silver, brass, and other metals are more easily found and less expensive than the figurals. Usually napkin rings are round, but oval, square and even diamond-shaped rings add a dash of variety. Polished brass, carved wood, and woven wicker rings are often found at flea markets, antique stores, estate sales, and other secondhand sales. Highly decorated with flowers, animals, or initials, these rings are priced from fifty cents to several dollars. There are even napkin rings that are specially designed for celebrations!

The holidays are a particularly good time for napkin ring collectors. Many companies produce napkin rings for Christmas, Easter, Thanksgiving, and other special days. Make sure to look for these seasonal rings at department, gift, and specialty stores during the holidays. In fact, if you wanted to, you could even specialize in holiday napkin rings.

Napkin rings are easy to display on shelves or in a decorative glass bowl, and they are very practical. Even if your family uses paper napkins at meal time, you can use your napkin rings. Once your collection is large enough, let each member of you family select a new napkin ring to use each week. If you help set the table, slip either a paper or a cloth napkin through the ring. People will be able to tell where they are sitting by finding the napkin ring that they chose for that week. If there is usually assigned seating at your dinner table, this can be a fun way to mix up the seating a bit. There's no better way to display your collection than to place them on the table at mealtime.

Napkin rings add a touch of elegance to any table setting. They can be an expression of one's personality, interest, hobbies—and seasonal napkin rings can help us enjoy the holidays a bit more. Napkin rings are fun to collect, and they can add a dash of elegance to any meal!

Related Collectibles: cloth napkins, place mats, tablecloths

61

Newspaper Clippings and Magazines

*"All the news
that's fit to print."*
Adolph Simon Ochs, 1858-1935

It would be difficult to find a less expensive or better collectible than newspaper clippings and magazines. These two collectibles cover almost any topic that you'd be interested in. They are plentiful, and they are easy to store and display. Both of these types of publications have been around for a long time, too.

The earliest recorded U.S. newspaper was published in Boston in 1690, and it was called *Public Occurrences both Foreign and Domestic*, and *The Saturday Evening Post* first rolled off of the presses in 1821. Ever since these first appearances, newspapers and magazines have become a staple of American life that can be found almost anywhere.

Walk down the newspaper isle in a good book store and you'll find dailies from Portland, Houston, New York, Boston, and many of the larger cities in the United States. If it's a very large newsstand, you might even see foreign papers from London, Paris, Tokyo, and other foreign financial centers.

The variety of magazines is even more staggering. There are thousands of general interest and specialty magazines covering everything from astronomy to zoos. There are magazines that specialize in antiques, baseball, cooking, sailing, toys, and just about anything else you can think of. Chances are, if you know what you want to be when you grow up, there's probably at least one magazine specifically written for that profession. There are even publications for those who have broader interests.

General interest magazines often include personality profiles, how to, self-help, recipes, and a variety of other article topics. This means that the options for a newspaper clipping or magazine collector are virtually unlimited.

In fact, you can assemble a collection of almost *anything* in the world through newspaper clippings and magazines. Are you interested in weather? All you have to do is scan the pages of a newspaper and clip out stories on snow storms, hurricanes, tornadoes, or other climatic phenomenon. How about collecting articles about heroes, places to travel, new discoveries, or sports? You might even clip and save advice, comics, recipes, crossword puzzles, horoscopes, or one of the other standard newspaper columns. Collecting clips from newspapers is not only fun, but it's also easy and inexpensive.

Ask your parents or friends to save their old newspapers for you. Once you've selected the area you want to specialize in, flip through the pages to see if there are any stories that will fit in your collection. Carefully cut out the articles and then decide how you want to arrange them.

One of the easiest ways to store and show a clipping collection is to keep them in a photo album or a scrapbook. Another way to keep a collection of clippings is to place them in manila folders which can be stored either in paper boxes or in a filing cabinet. Whichever method works for you—make sure that you keep up with it.

The worst thing a collector can face is a stack of crumpled clippings that have been jammed into a file. Chances are, if you fall too far behind, you'll eventually throw away the entire collection. If you keep it neat and orderly, though, you'll enjoy the collection for years to come.

Collecting magazines is a bit different from clipping articles. Collectors of clippings rely on recently published newspapers which tend to be thrown away after they're read. Magazine collecting, on the other hand, can mean either new or antique magazines—so the first question to ask yourself is whether or not you want to collect old or new publications. Although it might cost more to build a collection of older magazines, it's probably worth it. A collection of old magazines can help to document history, show changes in trends, and provide a window to the past. New magazines, on the other hand, help keep us informed of current events, styles, and personalities. Old or new, it's up to you.

Once you decide, you might want to specialize in a particular area. Some collectors specialize in magazines published in the year they were born. For example, someone who was born in 1990, might have *Smithsonian*, *Tiger Beat*, and the *Ladies Home Journal*. In a sense, this approach captures the life and times of the collector's birth year by documenting styles, trends, and news.

You could also build a collection that is subject-specific. A movie buff might collect *People*, *Entertainment Weekly*, *TV Guide*, or any general publication with feature stories highlighting the movie or entertainment industry. Some collectors choose their magazines based on the cover prints. Covers designed by famous artists such as Norman Rockwell or Maxfield Parrish are very popular. Many collectors build an entire collection based on a single magazine.

One of the most collectible magazines is *National Geographic*. Since the first issue came out in 1888, *National Geographic* magazine has taken the reader to the four corners of the globe. Whether in the South African desert, the Polar Caps, or the Everglades, *National Geographic* made us feel like we were there through clear, colorful photographs and compelling articles. That's perhaps, why collectors love to keep these popular magazines. With one of the longest consecutive runs in history, it would be nearly impossible to find every issue of *National Geographic*—but it sure would be fun to try.

National Geographic and other magazines can be purchased new or secondhand. Keep in mind that the older issues of any magazine can be scarce and can cost as much as $25 or more; however, more recent issues can be found at garage sales, "Friends of the Library" sales, flea markets, and used book stores for a few dollars or less. Don't forget to let your family and friends know that you're collecting magazines. They'll probably be more than happy to help you build your collection.

Magazines can be stored in reprint boxes, drawers, or in cardboard boxes. Select a few special magazines to display in Plexiglas frames and hang them on the wall, or set them on shelves. Magazines can even be laid flat on a table for browsing.

Collecting newspaper clippings or magazines is an interesting hobby. It can give us a glimpse into history or an in-depth look at a particular subject. Most of all, it's one hobby that's almost as affordable as it is fun!

Related Collectibles: books, pamphlets

62

Office Collectibles

....

*"When I was a lad I served a term as office boy to
an Attorney's firm. I cleaned the windows and I swept
the foor and I polished up the handle of the big front door.
I polished up that handle so carefullee that now
I am the ruler of the Queen's Navee!"*

Sir William Schwenck Gilbert, 1836-1911

W hen your father or grandfather first began working, their offices looked much different than the modern cubicles used in business today. Yesterday's modern office had a radiator heater for warming in the winter and a brass-bladed fan for cooling in the summer. Central heat and air conditioning didn't govern the business climate as it does today. Early offices had big wooden desks, possibly an oak swivel chair, and maybe even lawyer's bookcases. While the styles of these furnishings may have changed over the years, they're still found in most offices today. If you look at what was on the desk twenty or thirty years ago, though, chances are that much of the equipment is no longer used. It's the drastic changes in, or the disuse of, some office equipment which makes it so much fun to collect.

A candlestick telephone, an adding machine, a paperweight, and an assortment of fountain pens were standard issue for executive offices fifty years ago. An embossing machine with the company seal, rubber stamps, various paper clips and a stapler, could also be found. Any of these desk-top tools could make an interesting office equipment collection. The variety of old office collectibles is almost unlimited, and the supply is great—and there's more to most of them than meets the eye.

One of the most interesting office collectibles is the typewriter. This staple nineteenth century business machine was first patented in 1829 by William Austin Burt, who called his crude machine a typographer. A few years later, Burt's model was surpassed by a typewriter with the first movable keyboard. There are two broad classifications of typewriters—keyboard and index machines. Keyboard typewriters appeared first and are operated by depressing a key to type a letter or character. These machines were initially considered quite expensive, and sold for $100 or more, so a less expensive model was introduced.

131

The index typewriter had a dial with a list of all of the letters and characters. Each time a user wanted to type a particular letter, the dial was moved select it. This was a slow process, but it did provide a cheaper alternative to keyboard machines. Both kinds of typewriters come in many different styles. Eventually, however, index typewriters were phased out.

Unlike other old office collectibles such as telephones, paperweights, or inkwells, very few people collect typewriters, and since computers and electronic word processors have replaced standard typewriters, they are extremely affordable and easy to find. There are elegant cabinet, sturdy desk-top, and handy portable models. Some have modern keyboards with the characters and letters positioned where we would expect to find them, while others have mixed the alphabet up a bit in an effort to improve access. There are typewriters with changeable and specialty fonts including script. For those who don't have enough display space or interest in typewriters, there are several other office collectibles to consider.

Letter openers, slide rules, wooden yardsticks or rulers, and desk calendars were produced in enough variety to make an interesting collection. Specialize in a particular type of collectible, a specific era, or look for any office equipment that you find appealing. There's a large enough supply of old office equipment to support a variety of interests, and to create a wonderful display.

Most office collectibles display well on shelves, tables, or on desks, and some—including rulers, yardsticks, triangles, slide rules, and scissors—can be hung on the wall. Display your collection throughout the house, or create a single display in one corner of your room. Just make sure that you leave enough room for your collection to grow.

Old office collectibles are commonly found at garage sales, flea markets, church bazaars, estate sales, auctions, and "going out of business" sales. The most affordable collectibles tend to be those that attract the least number of collectors. Prices for these uncharted collectibles can range from twenty-five cents to a few dollars.

Office collectibles are a fun, almost unexplored area for young collectors. If these pre-automation relics are of interest to you, start looking now, and soon you'll be in business with a collection of your own!

Related Collectibles: advertisements

63

PATCHES

....

"A wandering minstrel I –
A thing of shreds and patches
Of ballads, songs, and snatches,
And dreamy lullaby!"
Sir William Schwenck Gilbert, 1836-1911

It may be surprising to learn that patches aren't only used to repair the worn spots in blue jeans. Patches are also decorative or symbolic pieces of fabric which can be sewn on uniforms or other clothing. Embroidered or printed patches come in a variety of shapes, sizes and colors. The number of patches and the subjects they include make them a great collectible for almost anyone.

Many different patches are worn on worker's uniforms. In fact, patches are such an integral part of uniforms, some people don't realize they're entirely separate. The repairman fixing the heater wears a patch with his company logo on his shirt. The waitress at the local restaurant has a patch sewn on her dress. The bus driver has a patch on his jacket. And the medic working on the ambulance wears a patch on her sleeve. Any one of these patches would make a fine addition to any collection, but there are many other patches to consider as well.

The branch, company, and unit that a soldier belongs to is identified by the patches he wears. Military patches are also worn to show rank, special teams, and accomplishments. For decades, military patches have drawn collectors to search for their prize. Surplus stores, military shows, antique stores, and even some auctions are likely spots for the military patch collector—but look for other patches, too.

Another closely related profession which uses patches is law enforcement. The police, sheriff's department, and state troopers wear a variety of patches. Departmental and American flag patches are often worn on the sleeves of law enforcement uniforms. Division, special team, unit citation, and other specialty patches may also be worn; however, it might be difficult for anyone not associated with law enforcement to collect these kinds of patches. Some states may restrict the ownership of law enforcement patches, badges, and uniforms to active or retired officers—but if your father or other relative is in law enforcement, they might be able to help you build up a pretty good patch collection.

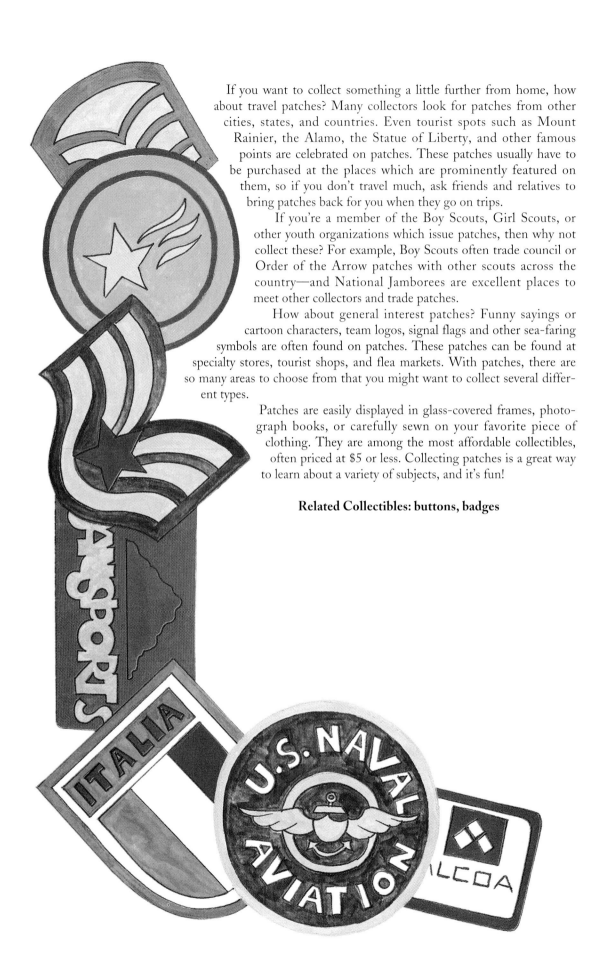

If you want to collect something a little further from home, how about travel patches? Many collectors look for patches from other cities, states, and countries. Even tourist spots such as Mount Rainier, the Alamo, the Statue of Liberty, and other famous points are celebrated on patches. These patches usually have to be purchased at the places which are prominently featured on them, so if you don't travel much, ask friends and relatives to bring patches back for you when they go on trips.

If you're a member of the Boy Scouts, Girl Scouts, or other youth organizations which issue patches, then why not collect these? For example, Boy Scouts often trade council or Order of the Arrow patches with other scouts across the country—and National Jamborees are excellent places to meet other collectors and trade patches.

How about general interest patches? Funny sayings or cartoon characters, team logos, signal flags and other sea-faring symbols are often found on patches. These patches can be found at specialty stores, tourist shops, and flea markets. With patches, there are so many areas to choose from that you might want to collect several different types.

Patches are easily displayed in glass-covered frames, photograph books, or carefully sewn on your favorite piece of clothing. They are among the most affordable collectibles, often priced at $5 or less. Collecting patches is a great way to learn about a variety of subjects, and it's fun!

Related Collectibles: buttons, badges

64

Pencils

························

"An incurable itch for scribbling takes possession of many, and grows inveterate in their insane breasts."
Decimus Junius Juvenal, 40-125

What better tool is there than a pencil for scribbling? On cold, wintry days when there's almost nothing to do, a pencil in hand can help while away the hours and spur creativity. Although most of us probably take them for granted, there are thousands of different kinds of pencils. Beyond the standard yellow, number two pencil, there are so many varieties that you might have fun just trying to count them.

The first lead pencils produced in the United States were manufactured by William Monroe. In 1812, this cabinetmaker from Concord, Massachusetts, crafted a timeless writing implement using domestic graphite. Today, the styles, colors, and messages printed on pencils make them a fun and inexpensive collectible for collectors of all ages.

Perhaps the most collectible pencils are those printed with advertising. Banks, stores, restaurants, and law firms are among the slew of businesses to use pencils as promotional items. Company names, logos, addresses and telephone numbers are often engraved on pencils to serve as constant reminders of the firms that gave them away. You can specialize in pencils from a particular type of business or collect as many different ones as you can.

Old advertising pencils can be found at flea markets, estate sales, and antique stores. There are two clues which may tell you if an advertising pencil is old. First, look at the address and see if a ZIP code is given. If there isn't a ZIP code, then the pencil was probably manufactured and printed prior to 1963. We know this because that is when the ZIP code came into use. The second clue requires a little more effort.

If you live in the same city as the business advertised on the pencil, you can do some research at the local library. Go to the reference desk and find out where the library keeps their old city directories. Then, look the business up in the directories, beginning with the most recent year, working your way back in time. Once you find the first and last year that the business was listed, you will have a range of time to date your pencil.

Another way to specialize is to only collect holiday pencils. For each holiday, discount and specialty stores roll out seasonal merchandise. Pencils are among the many items that receive special decals and colors to make them appropriately festive. Holiday pencils are decorated with bats, flags, turkeys, and shamrocks. Christmas pencils look scrumptious with red and white candy cane swirls, Easter pencils are pastel, and it's emerald isle green for Saint Patrick's Day.

Sometimes even the erasers get festive. Santas, pumpkins, snowmen, turkeys, sleighs, and Christmas trees top many holiday pencils. There are non-holiday-shaped erasers, too! Globes, dice, animals, cars, and others can be found. It might be somewhat more difficult to find these unique pencil toppers, but it's worth it.

How about collecting sports pencils? The National Football League teams are featured on specially licensed pencils as are the National Basketball Association, National Hockey League, and the National and American Baseball Leagues. Pick a favorite team or collect all of the sports pencils that come your way.

Also, mechanical pencils, especially the ones from the 1940s or later, are quite collectible. These early mechanical pencils are priced from $10 to several hundred depending upon age, design, and condition. Sometimes they are elegant, masculine, or just plain interesting to look at—and don't think for a moment that pencil collections can't be displayed.

Display pencils on tables, shelves, or on desks in a variety of ways. Place them in a cup with the point facing down to view their unique erasers. Jab pencils into a Styrofoam ball to admire most of the design. Or, lay them in a shallow, flat box to enjoy them from top to bottom.

Collecting pencils is fun and it will get you talking to a lot of people. So, get the lead out and start collecting pencils!

Related Collectibles: pencil sharpeners, pencil holders, pencil boxes

65

PENS

·················

*"A pen is certainly an excellent instrument to fix a
man's attention and to inflame his ambition."*

John Adams, 1735-1826

Many types of writing instruments have been used since man
first began to write. The Ancient Egyptians used reeds and
hollow pieces of bamboo to apply ink. Around 1000 B.C.,
the Chinese drew their symbols with camel's or rat's hair brushes.
Quills, which were introduced in Europe in the sixth century, were
used until the nineteenth century when they were replaced by
fountain pens. From these beginnings, came the forerunners of the
pens we use today.

Although the fountain pen was invented in the 1830s, it wasn't
commercially manufactured until about fifty years later. In 1888,
the first U.S. patent for a ballpoint pen was granted to John H.
Loud. Loud's pen was developed to write on rough surfaces, so it
didn't work very well on paper. Then, in 1944, Hungarian inventor Lazlo Biro invented the "Biro," the first ballpoint pen
designed to write on paper.

Since these early landmarks in the pen's history, hundreds of
different styles, colors, and designs have been manufactured.
Today, over 11 million fountain and more than 26 billion ballpoint pens are produced annually. The variety of designs is what
entices collectors to search for pens.

Many collectors specialize in a specific type of pen. Antique
fountain pens, for example, are very popular. These beautiful
writing instruments are made of polished metals, elegant woods,
and even hard rubber. Although the prices of early pens can be
high, it's worthwhile to familiarize yourself with them. Find out
what they look like, who made them, and what they're worth. Who
knows? You might find one of these treasures at a garage or rum-
mage sale someday.

Some collectors specialize in antique ballpoint pens, which can be
as elegant as the early fountain pens. Still others collect the old pen and
pencil sets which can cost $1,000 or more. For a young collector just start-
ing out, though, it's better to look for new pens.

There are several ways to specialize if you collect new pens. Among the more
collectible pens are the ones with animals, cartoon characters, or other unique figures

either painted, decaled, or molded to the pen itself. These pens tend to be available at discount and specialty stores. Also, there are pens with the names and logos of cities, states, and countries printed on them. These are especially nice souvenirs; however, the easiest type of pen to find and afford is the advertising pen.

Many businesses of all kinds, pay to have pens printed with their company logo, name, address, and telephone number, just so they can be given away. Probably many of the stores, banks, restaurants, and other businesses in your home town have some of these pens available. All you have to do is ask.

How about collecting pens from companies that are no longer in business? At garage and estate sales, you can sometimes buy an entire box full of old pens, pencils, and other office equipment for just a few dollars. Pull out the pens from businesses that are no longer around, and you will have a most unique collection to enjoy and display.

Display your pens in a flat, glass-covered cabinet or lying on a table or desk. To make a hanging display, sew loops on a cloth-covered board and slip each pen into a loop. While displaying pens might be a bit tricky, use your imagination and see what you come up with.

Collecting pens—whether antique or modern, can keep a collector occupied for a long time. The variety, availability, and affordability of pens means that almost anyone can enjoy collecting them. Over time, your collection might even grow to include finely crafted antique pens. Pens are a great choice for collectors of all ages—and you can write that in stone!

Related Collectibles: ink wells, pencils

66

Photographs

....

"One picture is worth a thousand words."
Fred R. Barnard, 1927-

Since 1888, when George Eastman introduced the first Kodak camera, taking pictures has become so easy that even a toddler can get a good shot. Forget setting the aperture, film speed, shutter speed and F-stop. With many of today's cameras, all you have to do is point and click.

Easy access to reasonably good quality photos has opened up a whole new area of collecting for anyone interested in capturing the moment. Compiling a collection of your own photographs may not seem like much when you begin, but as time goes by, you just might impress yourself.

Randomly shot photos of friends and places you've been don't necessarily make a collection. Instead, choose a specific topic and strive to take the definitive picture on the subject. For example, a collection of photographs of children might show them sleeping, eating ice cream, playing on a playground, getting a flu shot at the doctors, and watching a clown. These pictures, when taken together, could comprise a collection of children as seen through your eyes.

If you like scenery, how about a collection of snow-capped mountains? Take pictures of the snowy peaks of Mount Jefferson, Mount Bachelor, and Mount Ashland in Oregon to begin your collection. What you specialize in is up to you, but putting together a photograph collection of your work means more than just taking a lot of photographs.

Naturally, you have to follow through on the work that you've begun. Once the pictures are taken, the film will need to be developed. Select only the best shots from the developed roll and then find a way to organize them.

Write the location, the date, the names of the people in the picture, and any other appropriate information on the back of each photograph to keep a record. Then, decide how to display and store your pictures. Photograph albums are wonderful for displaying and storing pictures, but albums aren't the only way. While you may initially keep your collection in an album, it may eventually outgrow this method. Instead, you might want to purchase several file folders, large envelopes, or boxes.

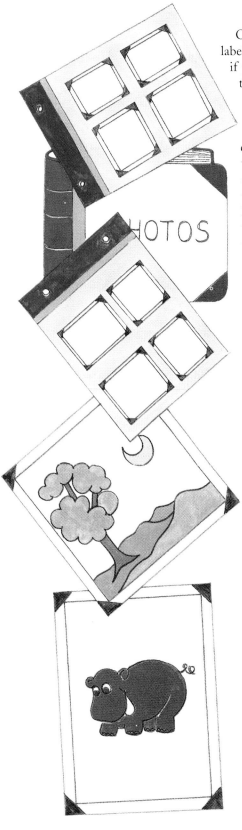

Once you decide what subjects to specialize in, you can label each folder, envelope, or box appropriately. For example, if you take pictures of children, as mentioned above, then the folders might be titled: "At Play," "At Work," "At Rest," and "Emotions." After all, an organized collection is enjoyable to look at and easy to maintain.

Building a collection of your own photographs is quite a bit of work, and it can be expensive—but if you're willing to put in the effort, and you can afford it, collecting photographs should bring you a great deal of satisfaction. Perhaps, someday, your photographs will be published in either a magazine or a book. Collecting photographs is a lot of fun, and if you like taking pictures, it's a snap.

Related Collectibles: historical photographs, camera equipment

67

PLACE MATS

····································

"For it's always fair weather
When good fellows get together
With a stein on the table and a good song ringing clear."
Richard Hovey, 1864-1900

Do you really like place mats? Do you have a favorite one that you eat dinner off of every night—or maybe several favorites you use throughout the week? Well, if you do, then you are like millions of other people. Place mats are an important part of many table settings, and they add a splash of color, a measure of beauty, and a dash of fun to any meal. The variety of styles, designs, and subjects make collecting place mats a great idea.

Place mats are made out of a variety of materials including cloth, plastic, straw, and many other natural and synthetic fibers. Mats are sewn, woven, printed, or crocheted. Lace, sequins, beads, glitter, and buttons decorate many of these plate holders. Everyone, from crafts people to large manufacturers, is making them.

With so many different kinds of place mats to choose from, you might want to specialize. Even though there are cotton, wicker, linen, and other elegant fabrics, the most popular place mats with young collectors are made out of plastic. There are basically two types of decorative plastic place mats. The first kind has the design printed directly on the plastic. The design on the second type is printed on paper and then laminated with plastic.

The great thing about plastic place mats is the variety of subjects printed on them. Buildings, cars, boats, cartoons, and bridges adorn them. Leaves, rocks and minerals, fish, and many other things are found in nature and on place mats. Set your plate on maps, musical instruments, toys, or clocks. In fact, there is a place mat for almost every topic. Perhaps, one of the most festive categories is the holiday place mat.

Holiday place mats are festive. Tom turkeys, frosty snowmen, fuzzy bunnies and other seasonal mats brighten up the holidays. Special holiday shapes like round pumpkins, leafy shamrocks, and the familiar outline of Santa's head make holiday place mats even more fun—and, they're easy to find. Look for holiday place mats at grocery, discount, specialty, gift, and other retail stores. If you buy them the day after each holiday, the prices will be low—

but if you would rather not pay for your place mats, then consider collecting restaurant place mats.

Diners, fast food, and specialty restaurants often have printed paper place mats. Sometimes these place mats are printed with the history of the restaurant, word games, or puzzles. Menus and local advertising are often featured on these useful mats. Since you might not want to use the paper place mats from your collection, you can either have them laminated for home use or placed in a Plexiglas frame to hang on the wall.

Collecting place mats is fun and affordable. Brighten up your dinner table and build an interesting collection with place mats!

Related Collectibles: cloth napkins, tablecloths, napkin rings

68

PLANTS

....

"He that plants trees loves others beside himself."
Thomas Fuller, 1654-1734

If you want to build a collection that can really grow into something special, then collect plants. There are over 200,000 different species of plants, many of which can be cultivated. Plants are not only an important part of our ecosystem, they're also beautiful to look at.

Before deciding what kinds of plants to collect, you should determine what the growing conditions are where you live. For example, if you live in Florida or Southern California where there are few killing frosts, then you might have a choice of keeping your plants either inside or outside. If, on the other hand, you live in upstate New York where the snow drifts are several feet deep, keeping your plants inside, where the temperature is regulated by a thermostat, might be best.

Once the growing conditions have been considered, either borrow a good plant or gardening book from the library or purchase one at a bookstore. Flip through the pages to see what kind of plants you like the best. Then, go down to a local gardening store and talk with a knowledgeable clerk.

Each plant requires a different level of care. Some need to be placed in a warm room with direct sunlight, others need to be shaded. Many plants need to be pruned, have their leaves sprayed, and some need food or fertilizer. Some plants must be started by seed while others can take root from a cutting. All of this information should be available either in the plant book, or by talking with the clerk at the garden store. You'll need to know at least some of this information before deciding what type of plants to collect.

Among the most popular plants for indoor gardeners are cacti and other succulents. Interesting shapes and ornate flowers make these plants especially appealing. Both cacti and other succulents grow slowly and require a minimum level of care. Infrequent watering, moderate sunlight, and occasional fertilizing make this a low-maintenance choice.

Cacti and other succulents can be purchased at grocery, department, or garden stores. The prices vary depending upon the kind of plant, the size, and the type of planter that the cacti comes in. Expect to pay $3.00 or more for a plant of any size. If your collection is on a small budget, consider starting your collection with a few cuttings.

Taking cuttings from live cacti and succulents, especially hybrids, provides a quick, easy, and inexpensive means of growing new plants. Look up the various methods of propagation depending upon the type of plants you're trying to grow. Then ask permission before taking any cuttings.

Other popular plants to consider collecting include ivy, flowers, ferns, and herbs which can be used in cooking. Empty plastic or paper milk containers can be used as planters, and with your parents permission, soil can be taken from your own backyard for a very inexpensive collection.

Collecting plants and learning how to care for them can be a wonderful experience. Do a little research and decide if a living collection will fit in with your interests and ability to care for it. While plants might not be an obvious collectible, they can grow on you!

Related Collectibles: flowerpots, books and prints with plants

69

PLATES

....

*"Them that has china plates themsels is the maist
careful no to break the china plates of others."*
Sir James Matthew Barrie, 1860-1937

Plates are among the oldest collectibles. It's possible that your mother has decorative plates hanging on the wall, displayed in the china hutch, or propped up on a shelf. Perhaps she collected the plates herself, or maybe they were inherited from her mother or grandmother. Plates with beautiful flowers, birds, city scapes, or those that commemorate an event or anniversary make wonderful collectibles.

There is an endless variety to consider. There are almost as many different kinds of plates as there are collectors. You can collect plates based on their age, manufacturer, design, or use. For example, some collectors only look for plates that are very old. Redware plates, which date from the 1600s, although expensive, are highly sought after. The price for a good Redware plate can run anywhere from $100 to several thousands. Fortunately, though, you don't have to spend this kind of money to find older plates worth collecting.

One of the most common collectible plate is the calendar plate. Calendar plates were popular from about 1905 to 1930, although they are still being made today. Decorated with animals, flowers, pretty ladies, and, of course, the twelve months of the year, calendar plates are great collectibles. In their early days, calendar plates were sometimes given away as advertising premiums. This means that you may find a few with a company name or logo printed on either the front or back. Calendar plates show up with great frequency at flea markets, antique shops and auctions. Prices for calendar plates can range any where from a few dollars to thirty or more. The most popular calendar plates are those dated before 1905 or after 1930, with the highest prices placed

on older plates. While some enthusiasts collect only plates from their birth year, others try to build up a collection of continuous years.

Another way to focus your efforts is to collect any and all plates made by a specific manufacturer. For example, some collectors search for Wedgwood, Lenox, or with a Western flair—Wallace China. To these collectors, it doesn't matter if the designs match or not. Often, a beautiful collection representing a company's finest work can be assembled. For those wishing to gather matching plates, look for specific patterns.

For example, many collectors enjoy collecting Fiesta ware. This colorful dinnerware was manufactured in eleven different colors. Although many collectors try to assemble an entire set of a specific color, you could, instead, collect one or two plates of each color. This rainbow collection can be displayed or used for special occasions. Additional collectible designs include Currier & Ives, Willow Ware, and a never-ending list of other distinctive patterns.

You could collect advertising, limited edition, travel, or plates printed with specific topics such as holidays, animals, scenic views, or religious plates. The only limits are the collector's preferences and the cost of the plates.

Finally, some collectors specialize based upon the intended use of the plate. For example, desert plates, regardless of age, manufacturer, or design are collected. Also, bread, serving, and shaped plates are highly sought after.

Collectible plates have had a huge following for many years. Often, a collector will start with plates and then begin collecting cups, saucers, and the rest of the set. However you decide to begin your collection, there's one thing that's certain, collecting plates can dish up a lot of fun!

Related Collectibles: cups, saucers, and drinking glasses

70

Playing Cards

··

"True luck consists not in holding the
best of the cards at the table:
Luckiest he who knows just when to rise and go home."
John Milton Hay, 1838-1905

Awritten record dates the existence of cards in Europe to as early as fourteen B.C.; however, some varieties of Chinese and Indian cards might be even older than that. Originally dealt solely for the purpose of playing games of chance, cards became popular in the eighteenth century for forecasting the future. Although the fortune-telling tarot cards hold interest for some collectors, playing cards have more universal appeal.

The invention of the printing press in the fifteenth century saw the use of playing cards expand. The greatest variation can be found among the earliest cards. Playing cards of all shapes and sizes, with a variety of face and number styles, were printed by many different companies. In fact, a study of playing cards over the years may provide a window to the past.

Art, literature, and politics were popular topics for decks of cards. When kings and queens were out of favor with their royal subjects, they were replaced in the deck by commoners. Military officers took their posts as face cards during times of war—and in the United States, the faces of presidents and Indian chiefs were favored instead of the monarchy. Flip the card over, and even the back tells a story.

Marble designs and colored woodcut patterns of the nineteenth century were the earliest attempts to decorate the backs of cards. Later, pictures of royalty, art work, country scenes, and many other interesting subjects appeared. Today, there are several hundred or more back cover designs. In fact, many collectors base entire collections on these designs alone.

Everything from airplanes to zoos have been featured on the backs of playing cards. Among the most popular and easiest to find are advertising decks. Dog food, tires, magazines, soda pop, and other products appear on the flip-side of cards. Many collectors select one or two areas to specialize in. For example, transportation cards are a popular collecting category. Playing

cards that once helped airline, steamship, and railroad passengers pass the time, are highly sought after by collectors.

Collecting souvenir decks is also a common specialty. Many collectors look for cards from world fairs, stage plays, expos, concert tours, or other major events. Also, colleges, museums, and several tourist attractions appear on playing cards. If you enjoy sports, look for cards with the names and logos of your favorite teams printed on them. Decks with politics, fine arts, and interesting designs are also fair game. In fact, the options are almost unlimited.

The great thing about collecting cards is that, as long as your specialty isn't too obscure, you can find them almost anywhere. Old decks turn up at flea markets, antique shows, and paper shows. Modern decks with a variety of subjects can be found at department, gift, and hobby stores. You might not even have to leave the house to get started. Special offers on the backs of cereal boxes or other household products sometimes include decks of advertising cards.

Some collectors even specialize in a single card, collecting only jokers, from many different decks. Since the joker cards are hardly ever used, they're usually found in good condition. There are probably hundreds, if not thousands, of different styles of jokers. You may even find some in your house—tucked away in packs of forgotten playing cards.

Collecting playing cards is easy and interesting—so deal yourself a handful of fun, and collect cards!

Related Collectibles: card games

71

Pocketknives

....

*"Fingers were made before forks,
and hands before knives."*

Jonathan Swift, 1667-1745

In 1819, the first of what would become over 100 U.S. knife factories or cutleries were opened in Worcester, Massachusetts. It wasn't until the 1960s, though, that knife collecting caught on. When manufacturers began labeling each knife with the country of origin, collectors took notice. Collectors and dealers began stockpiling the older, unmarked knives believing they would increase in value. While this has proved true, interest in collecting new pocketknives has also grown.

Pocketknives come in a wide variety of styles and sizes, and though steel blades are standard, knife handles are made out of many different materials. Wood, plastic, ivory, and metal have been fashioned into handles on highly collectible pocketknives. Some are decorative (with carving, scrimshaw, decals, or metal stamps affixed to them), while others are very plain.

Some pocketknives are advertising pieces, with the names of companies and logos stamped on them. These are prized by both advertising and knife collectors who compete for the older knives; however, recent advertising knives are usually made in such large quantities that they're easy to find. These should be especially appealing to new collectors.

Another popular type of pocketknife is the gadget knife. Swiss Army knives are probably the most famous gadget knives. Corkscrews, fingernail files, bottle openers, toothpick tweezers, scissors, screwdrivers, and other tools may be included. Pocketknives designed with the camper in mind are also treasured. Spoons, forks, compasses, saws, rulers, magnifying glasses, can openers, and other utensils can be found in these outdoor versions.

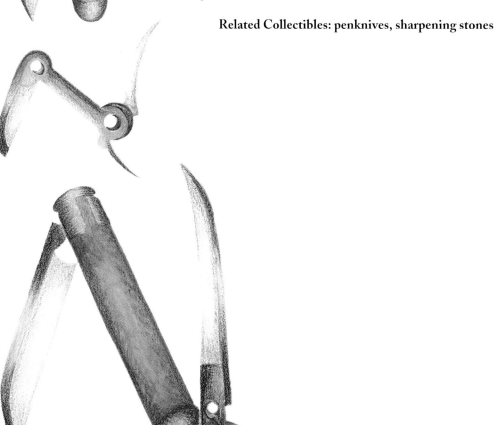

Even if you begin your pocketknife collection with new knives, eventually you might become interested in the older ones. Antique pocketknives are sold at flea markets, antique shows, gun shows—and, every once and a while at other secondhand sales. Before you start looking for old knives, however, you need to become familiar with them.

First, get a good reference guide and learn about the manufacturers, styles, and values. Before buying any knives, look at as many of them as possible. Prices vary greatly, and if you don't keep up with current values, you might pay too much. Also, there are many collector's clubs which you may find both helpful and fun to join. Sometimes these clubs have swap meets where pocketknives are sold and traded. This is a great way to learn about your new hobby—and you might even get a few ideas on how to exhibit your new collection.

Pocketknives are often displayed by laying them down on cloth-covered boards and tying them in place with a thin wire. This makes an attractive presentation, especially if the board is hung on the wall to be viewed; however, pocketknives can also be nicely displayed on a shelf or table. Just make sure the knives are out of reach for any little brothers or sisters.

Keep in mind that pocketknives are not toys. They should be handled carefully, according to the rules your parents set down—and it's probably a good idea not to open the blades without adult supervision.

There are a variety of knives, and if you decide to collect them, you'll have a pocket full of fun!

Related Collectibles: penknives, sharpening stones

72

Political Items

Items

....

"Public life is regarded as the crown of a career,
and young met it is the worthiest ambition.
Politics is still the greatest and the most honorable adventure."

John Buchan, the Lord Tweedsmuire, 1875-1940

Collectors are wild about politics. In American politics, candidates running for everything from dogcatcher to president, have generated a treasure trove of political collectibles. Winning candidates, and even those taking second or third place, spread their message with pamphlets, stickers, ribbons, and many other political give-a-ways. Collectors, young and old, can help preserve history, learn about the past, and have a great time collecting political items.

The most collectible political items relate to significant politicians or historical events—and while the winner's campaign items hold a great deal of interest, so do some of the "almost-wons." Colorful personalities such as Gary Hart, Jesse Jackson, and Ross Perot attract the attention of collectors. Each of them, like their predecessors, used a massive amount of paper, plastic, wood, rubber, metal, and cloth, to take their case to the people.

Ribbons, pens, watches and fobs, pocketknives, neckties, medals, coins, and other items are printed and plastered with the smiling faces of candidates. Even with so many items to choose from, though, the most popular political collectible has to be pin-back buttons.

Political buttons became popular in 1896 when Presidential hopeful William McKinley used them extensively in his campaign. McKinley's bid for the Presidency marked the beginning of mass-produced political buttons, and they have been the cornerstone of politicking ever since.

Among the most scarce buttons are those from the 1920 and 1924 presidential campaigns of James Cox and John W. Davis. While the values listed for these and other highly sought after buttons range from several hundred to well over two thousand dollars, the prices of other buttons are much more reasonable.

The values listed for common buttons range anywhere from a few dollars to over $50, depending upon the candidate, the age, and rarity

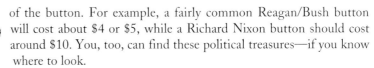

of the button. For example, a fairly common Reagan/Bush button will cost about $4 or $5, while a Richard Nixon button should cost around $10. You, too, can find these political treasures—if you know where to look.

The best places to find old political items are at flea markets, antique shows, and collector events; however, garage and estate sales can sometimes be good sources as well. Before beginning the search, pick up a reliable price guide to familiarize yourself with current values. If you collect political pens, review the prices for all the pens listed. While you may not find any of the pens listed in the price guide, you'll at least have a range of values.

Collecting political items is a fun and interesting way to keep and learn a bit about history. As you build your collection, don't overlook the new memorabilia coming out of today's local, state, and national campaigns. Remember: Today's campaign button is tomorrow's collectible. Start your collection today, and it won't be politics as usual anymore!

Related Collectibles: military collectibles

73

Postcards

······································

*"She'll wish there was more, and that's the
great art o' letter-writin'."*
Charles Dickens, 1812-1870

Postcards are second only to stamps as the most popular paper collectible. Postcards are often thought of as an "all encompassing" collectible because almost every subject known to man has, in some form, been printed on a postcard. Perhaps that's why collecting postcards has become so popular!

In 1869, Emmanuel Herrman, printed the first known postcard in Austria. His invention sparked a frenzy of communication which, in a single dose, lasts no longer than ten sentences: "Wish you were here," "Having a great time," "Daddy caught a big fish, but it got away." The messages scribbled on the backs of postcards are almost as varied as the cards themselves— but it's usually the picture printed on the front of the card that piques the collector's interest.

Some say the popularity of postcards soared after their appearance at the Colombian Exposition of 1892. Various scenes from the exposition were printed on postcards, and mailed to family and friends. Early collectors begin their collection with the first postcard they received. It was almost assumed that the postcard would be treasured forever. "Here's another card for your collection" was often written on the backs of old postcards. Today, with so many different cards to choose, it's helpful to specialize.

Many collectors specialize in postcards with specific topics or themes. For example, sports, transportation, and advertising are very popular. Postcards with city scapes, country views, mountains, and beaches are widely collected. Plants, animals, and other natural wonders are common. Collectors of holiday cards might even specialize in postcards from a specific day. Collecting Christmas, Halloween, Independence Day, or Easter postcards could keep a collector busy for many years and result in quite a nice collection.

Another interesting collection might only include recipes. New postcards with regional recipes printed on them can be found almost everywhere. Ice cream, specialty cookies, chili, and many other foods are on the menu for postcard collectors. If you already collect something else, then you might want to begin collecting postcards which relate to your current collection.

For example, a marble collector in Virginia collects postcards which feature Marblehead, Massachusetts. A kitchenware collector

might look for cards with recipes, kitchen utensils, or any subject related to cooking. Character collectors should enjoy collecting postcards printed with animated cartoon characters, and stamp collectors should be able to find many postcards of interest to them. Collecting postcards is a great way to supplement and enhance almost any collection.

After you decide what kind of postcard to collect, you get to look for them. New postcards can be found at most stores that cater to tourists. Gift shops, service stations, drugstores, and even supermarkets are likely sources. Old postcards aren't that difficult to find, but you do have to know where to look.

Antique shows, flea markets, and paper shows are among the most reliable places to shop for old postcards; however, auctions and even garage sales can be surprisingly good as well. Depending upon the age, subject, and condition of a postcard, you can expect to pay anywhere from a few cents to a few dollars for each card—and very rare postcards sometimes sell for $50 or more.

Although you will no doubt have to buy some cards for your collection, don't overlook the obvious "free" sources. Parents and grandparents often have postcards tucked away in drawers or stacked on shelves, and friends who travel might have access to a number of interesting postcards. Mention your collecting interests, and perhaps you'll have help making your collection grow.

A growing collection needs to be both displayed and organized. Postcards are often framed, or arranged in photograph or scrap albums. Display them on tables, shelves, or hang them on the wall. When the entire collection becomes too large to display, store most of the cards in a shoe box and exhibit only a few at a time.

The options for postcard collectors are endless. The list of different subjects could fill the pages in this entire book—so decide what to specialize in and get started!

Related Collectibles: greeting cards

74

POSTERS

....

"Nature hath made one world, and art another."
Sir Thomas Browne, 1605-1682

Posters have come a long way since the simple designs of early hand-bills and broadsides. Yesterday's square print and line drawings have been replaced by hundreds of different lettering types, detailed draw-ings, and bold, colorful photography. Many posters are artistic creations which not only communicate a message, but also entice collectors to seek their beauty.

The development of color lithography was the catalyst for the production of early nineteenth century posters. French advertising, American circus, and military posters are among the most collectible. These examples of printing history are highly sought after and are usually very expensive. As with so many other paper collectibles, the number of subjects and the values are as varied as the collectors themselves.

Choosing an area to specialize in can be difficult for poster col-lectors. Travel, sports, advertising, and politics are just a few of the subjects which frequently appear on posters today. Depending upon your interests, you might collect posters from several different cate-gories.

One of the most popular areas of collecting is posters from the big screen. Ever since the first movie was shown on a public screen in 1896, there's been a wide variety of posters touting everything from animation to westerns. These posters announced not only the name of the film, but also the producer, film company, and the actors who starred in the film. Depending upon when a film was produced, who the actors are, and what the film's about, a movie poster can be valued anywhere from a few dollars up to several thousand. Today, the affordable movie posters tend to be the ones that can be purchased as souvenirs. Specialty stores are the best places to look for these modern posters. Actual lobby posters are difficult to find and are among the most expensive.

Old movie, advertising, military, circus, and other specialty posters are sold at antique shows, auctions, flea markets, and paper shows. The price of a given poster

should be based upon age, rarity, design, coloration, condition, and subject matter. Before investing more than just a few dollars in old posters, you should buy a good price guide to become familiar with current values—and, if you decide to collect new posters, there are at least two ways to find them.

If you know someone connected with a particular industry that generates posters, ask them to help you. Teachers, librarians, safety officers, engineers, and many other professionals receive posters from their national associations. Once these posters have served their purpose, you might be able to get them for your collection. The other option is to collect commercially produced posters.

There are thousands of posters printed each year for decorating our walls. Posters of famous people, exotic places, and current events can be found at many retail stores. These usually cost less than $10 and can be as much fun to collect as the early posters. Sports, inspirational, and famous personalities are among the most common. If you want something that tickles your funny bone, why not collect humorous posters? Any poster that makes you laugh or giggle is fair game.

Collecting posters is great fun and the list of subjects is almost endless. If you want an affordable collectible that can decorate your entire room, then consider posters—they're fantastic.

Related Collectibles: lobby cards, prints, advertising

75

Pull Toys

....

"I will make you brooches and toys for your delight
Of bird song at morning and starshine at night."
Robert Louis Stevenson, 1850-1894

Wheeled pull toys carved out of white limestone date from 12 B.C. These Persian playthings were crafted into animal shapes for young children to play with. Later versions were fashioned out of stuffed fabric, wood, porcelain, metal and plastic. The subjects for pull toys range from animals to trucks and everything in between. It's the variety and the playability of these amusements that make them great collectibles for the young and the young at heart.

In the mid-1800s, pull toys were very popular. Elaborate bell toys featuring animals, people, and make-believe creatures rang through the hall at the tug of a string. Other pull toys either obeyed silently, or the faint sound of a head bobbing up and down could be heard. These appealing toys were dragged across fields, through mud puddles, and over river banks. They went everywhere their young masters commanded and endured tough treatment. For this reason, early pull toys are quite rare and expensive. Although they're not within most of our budgets, we can enjoy them through pictures in books or in antique price guides. Don't be discouraged if the old toys are out of your reach, there are many new pull toys to collect.

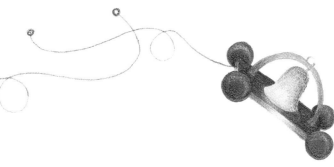

Probably the most famous pull toys produced during the past forty years are the wooden figures manufactured by Fisher-Price. Dogs, ducks, elephants, and other animals have been fashioned into the best pull-arounds that a tot could hope for. The early all-wooden toys, and those which feature Disney characters, are among the most desirable; however, non-character toys made after 1949 are easier to find and are more affordable. These recent pull toys which were manufactured with some plastic parts, can be found at resale shops, church bazaars, and garage sales for just a few dollars—and since Fisher-Price still manufactures pull toys, collectors can buy them in mint condition, for $30 or less.

Another famous line of pull toys are the coiled Slinky toys. James Industries manufactures a seal, kitten, worm, frog, and a few other plastic spring-loaded toys. Although not all of them are mounted on wheels, these spring toys can really move. When the front part of the toy is pulled forward and the spring is stretched, the back part soon follows. It almost looks as if the toy is hopping forward as the spring snaps the two ends together.

Many other pull toys are being crafted by toy makers who sell their playthings at craft shows and festivals. These, too, make great additions to any pull toy collection. Before you begin collecting, though, do a little research.

Walk down the isles of the best toy store in town and see what kind of new pull toys are on the shelves. Chances are that, in addition to the ones mentioned here, you'll find cars, trains, wagons, and more. Also, look in a good price guide to see what values are listed for Fisher-Price and other old pull toys. Once you've done your homework, you can decide what type of pull toys to collect.

Whether on wheels or pulled along by coils, pull toys are great! Just look to see what's available and then move forward with your new collection.

Related Collectibles: push and wind-up toys

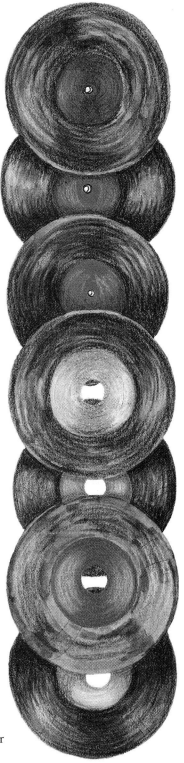

76

RECORDS, TAPES, AND COMPACT DISCS

···

*"A unalterable and unquestioned law of the musical world
required that the German text of French operas sung by
Swedish artists should be translated into Italian for the clear
understanding of English-speaking audiences."*
Edith Wharton, 1862-1937

Thomas Alva Edison invented the phonograph in 1877, and
ever since, many different kinds of recordings have been produced. Instrumental and vocal music, poetry, stories, and even
bird calls have been recorded for listeners to learn from and enjoy. In
fact, the variety of recordings is so huge, that even the thousands of
books which have been written on the subject, don't even cover the
topic.

There are so many different types of recordings, ranging from
advertising to waltzes, that collectors must specialize in order to have a
manageable hobby. Before you decide what kind of recordings to specialize in, however, you must decide what you want them recorded on.

Phonograph records are probably the most commonly collected
recordings—and for good reason. If taken care of, records will last a
very long time. Most of the early classics are only available on vinyl,
and for many, records are "the next best thing to being there." These
are good reasons to collect records, but there's a catch: You need a
working record player to enjoy the 33-1/3-, 45- or 78-rpm recordings.
If you have such a machine, and old recordings are of interest to you,
then collecting records makes sense.

If you don't have a record player but still want to collect some of
the old material, then cassette tapes might be the answer. Tapes have
been around for more than twenty years, and there have been a lot of
good recordings on tape; however, the best reason to collect cassettes is
that you might be able to get a friend to tape records or compact discs for

you. This way, you get the best of both recorded worlds. Keep in mind, though, that tapes are relatively fragile and may not last as long as records or compact discs.

Finally, if you're only interested in modern recordings, then compact discs are probably the best choice. Compact discs are the preferred choice of many listeners and almost everything being released is on compact disc. The prices for compact disc players have come down and there are portable, carousel, and in-the-dash models.

If you decide to collect records, there's an amazing variety of recordings to choose from. Many collectors look for limited release recordings including advertising, instructional, or unique entertainment records. Early advertisers produced holiday and promotional records that are now quite collectible. Also, special albums which teach a language, how to repair something, how to dance, or how to identify birds by their calls are also of interest. Finally, albums recorded by celebrities such as Patty Duke, Star Trek's William Shatner, and Mayberry's George Lindsay are highly sought after.

Old country, jazz, humor, and blues recordings appeal to many collectors. Also, many albums are collected for the album cover's art work. Elaborate, funky, or just plain weird art on the cover of an old record album almost insures that some collector will scoop it up.

Old records can be found at garage sales, auctions, flea markets, and at record shows which are held in cities across the country. Depending upon who made the album, what kind of recording it is, the condition, and what the cover looks like, the price can range anywhere from twenty-five cents to well over $100 dollars. Keep in mind that records bought at record shows or shops tend to be much more expensive than those sold at garage sales.

Collecting tapes usually means either buying new commercially produced tapes or making the tapes yourself. If you decide to buy commercially produced tapes, keep in mind that tapes may not last as long as records or compact discs. A better choice might be to ask a friend to make tapes of records and compact discs that you borrow from the local library or from other friends. Although these tapes will probably wear out long before the records or compact discs that they were recorded from, the advantages will be the very low cost to build a collection and the flexibility that taping both records and compact discs will give you.

Collecting compact discs usually means that only modern recordings will be collected. If, for example, you are interested in collecting "New Country" or "Rap" music, then compact discs are an excellent choice. Certainly many other categories including opera, jazz, blues, classical, and humor are open to compact disc collectors. Although some selected older material is becoming available on compact disc, keep in mind that the choices are still limited.

Recordings on all three media can be found at church bazaars, flea markets, and other secondhand sales; however, condition is very important. When you buy used cassettes or compact discs you might be disappointed. It's generally easier to spot scratches or warping on records if you look close enough. Before buying expensive secondhand recordings, it's wise to get a price guide to become familiar with current values.

Recorded material is different from a lot of other categories in that it requires a certain climate in order to survive. Moderate temperatures, no direct sunlight, and a dust-free environment will help preserve your recordings for years to come.

Whether you decide to collect records, tapes, or compact discs, it's certain you'll find many hours of listening enjoyment and entertainment through your collection.

Related Collectibles: radios, sheet music, instruments

Refrigerator Magnets

"Seek roses in December, ice in June."
Lord Byron, 1788-1824

There was a time when wintry ice from lakes and ponds was cut, hauled, and stored beneath the ground to preserve food for long periods of time. This was before ice boxes or refrigerators were invented. A time when ice in June was as rare as roses in December. Today, a refrigerator without at least one decorative magnet clinging to the front is even more scarce than Lord Byron's roses or ice.

Ice boxes, which were cooled with large blocks of ice, were replaced in the 1920s with refrigerators. This meant that food could be kept longer than ever before, and it set the stage for one of the most fun collectibles around—refrigerator magnets.

The popularity of refrigerator magnets surprises many, but the reasons are quite simple. Refrigerator magnets are inexpensive souvenirs and gifts, most collectors have a perfect place to display them right in their own kitchen, and the variety of subjects covered will keep even the most active collector busy.

There are probably thousands of different types of refrigerator magnets. Elephants, pigs, flowers, cars, buildings, trains, and even fine art hang on refrigerators all over the world. In fact, the subjects are as varied as the people who collect them. Chances are, you already have the beginnings of a collection in your home.

Go look on your refrigerator. Are there any decorative or photograph magnets stuck to the door? If there are, then you and your family have already begun collecting! Just decide what kind of magnets you like, and start adding to the collection.

One of the most interesting and affordable types of refrigerator magnets are the free advertising magnets given away by businesses. The creative shapes and slogans featured on business magnets make them desirable. A giant tooth reminds us to schedule our next dental check-up, the 1957 Chevy steers us to the mechanic for repairs, a Band-Aid keeps the hospital number close at hand, and a birthday cake with the telephone number of a favorite bakery looks delicious. These magnets and countless others are yours for the asking. Most businesses are more than happy to give you one of their promotional refrigerator magnets.

How about collecting travel magnets? The subjects of travel magnets include tourist attractions, historical sites, cities, states, and countries you might visit. The great thing about travel magnets is that family members and friends can easily send them to you or bring them back from their trips. They don't weigh much and they hardly take up any room.

Other areas to consider are holiday, animal, transportation, art, or sport magnets. Some enthusiasts only collect magnets which are handmade and sold at craft fairs. Others find their collectibles at gift, grocery, or department stores. Refrigerator magnets are not difficult to find, but picking an area to specialize in can be. Some people just collect whichever ones that they happen to like.

Collecting refrigerator magnets is fun and it's one collectible that will stick with you for a very long time!

Related Collectibles: magnets, bottle openers

78

Restaurant Collectibles

*"My advice to you is not to inquire
why or whither, but just enjoy your ice cream while it's
on your plate - that's my philosophy."*
Thornton Niven Wilder, 1897-1975

The highlight of any week is eating at a favorite restaurant. Whether it's Mexican, Italian, Chinese, or even home-style cuisine, it always seems to taste better when someone else chops, mixes, stirs, and bakes. Although restaurants remain extremely popular today, they are not new establishments. Public eating places have existed in some form since ancient times, with the modern version appearing in the eighteenth century. What's relatively new about restaurants is their contribution to collecting.

When some people think about restaurant collectibles, they instantly think about the toys which are included in kids' meals at fast food restaurants. These are without a doubt, some of the best restaurant collectibles available. Ever since they were first introduced, the toy surprises in a burger or taco lunch have steadily improved to become the best part of the meal.

Dolls, cars, puzzles, games and coloring books are the treasured prizes in these entertaining meals. Toys that roll, spin, bob up and down, or make a noise, make dining out more fun than ever before. Some of the playthings even feature characters from popular movies or television shows. At prices of $3 or less, the kid's meals with a collectible enclosed are great buys, but they aren't the only restaurant collectibles.

Many family, diner, and trendy restaurants sell promotional T-shirts, mugs, baseball caps and other items with the name, logo, and address of the restaurant printed on them. While the prices range anywhere from a few dollars to over $20, these, too, are great collectibles.

If older restaurant collectibles are of interest, then there are even more options. Cups, plates, glasses, serving trays and other printed items used in restaurants that have long been out of business, show up at antique shops, auctions, flea markets and other secondhand sales. Also, signs which hung in the restaurants to advertise which coffee, ice cream, or bread was being served are also quite popular. Prices range from a few dollars to several hundred depending upon what the item is, what restaurant it came from, and the item's age and condition.

For restaurant collectibles at no or low cost, consider some of the following options. Paper or laminated menus make wonderful restaurant collectibles. A menu collection begun ten years ago, would be fun to look at to see what the prices were. Many restaurant managers are more than happy to provide a young collector with a menu at no cost—but if menus are hard to come by, then try collecting paper placemats, calendars, matchbook covers, coasters, or other items with the restaurant's name, logo, and address printed on them. Any of these free collectibles can put you on the path to a great restaurant collection.

Building a collection of restaurant items can be the foundation to expand into other areas, or it can be a great collection by itself. Regardless of how your collection develops, restaurant collectibles are delicious!

Related Collectibles: advertising, kitchenware

79

Salt and Pepper Shaker Sets

"Before you trust a man, eat a peck of salt with him."
Anonymous

To put a little spice into your life, how about collecting salt and pepper shaker sets? While shaker sets are very common on today's dinner table, the variety of sets available are anything but run of the mill. That's what attracts so many collectors to salt and pepper shakers.

Salt and pepper shakers come in a variety of shapes and sizes. They're made out of many different materials. Plastic, wood, metal, glass, chalk, china, Plexiglas, marble, leather, and just about any other material you can think of has probably been used to make shakers. While cut crystal and gold trimmed sets are beautiful, the salt and pepper shakers that attract the attention of most collectors are the novelty sets.

Among the most popular novelty shakers are the figural sets. Cows, ducks, monkeys, fish, dogs, cats, and many other animals are highly sought after. Holiday figurals including Santa, snowmen, pumpkins, flags, bunnies, and other seasonal shakers are also treasured. There have also been a great number of sets with Disney and other well-loved characters.

If the variety of figures isn't enough to pique your interest, then the styles should. "Go along" shaker sets have two differently shaped shakers that are somehow related. For example, one shaker might be a lock and the other a key. Other shaker sets fit or nest together. For example, a donkey shaker may contain the salt

while the saddle bag resting on the donkey's back holds the pepper. There are shakers that squeak, move, dangle, and even nod. These unique shaker sets are among the most desirable and they are a lot of fun to collect.

Another option is advertising shakers. Many businesses, cities, states, countries, and tourist attractions are featured on salt and pepper shakers. These sets often appeal to general advertising and travel collectors. With increased competition, advertising salt and pepper shakers are becoming difficult to find and somewhat expensive. If you look hard enough, though, there are still a few good ones around.

Flea markets, garage sales, antique shops, and collectibles shows are the best places to find used or antique novelty shakers. Prices range anywhere from a few dollars to well over $200, depending upon the subject, style, age, and condition.

Before you start collecting older shakers, it's a good idea to get a hold of a good price guide to see what's available and what the values are. Become familiar with the information in the guide, talk with knowledgeable dealers, and if possible—join a collector's club. The more you learn about salt and pepper shaker sets, the better choices you will make as you build your collection.

Another option, which requires less research, is to collect new shakers. New novelty salt and pepper shaker sets are available at grocery, department, and gift stores. Prices are generally in the $5 to $20 range.

Collecting salt and pepper sets, especially the figural shakers is a lot of fun. Add a pinch of seasoning to your life, and start collecting shakers today!

Related Collectibles: open salts, sugar shakers

SCARVES and NECKTIES

"Clothes make the man."

Attributed to Samuel Langhorne Clemens (Mark Twain), 1835-1910

Scarves and neckties are two clothing accessories which can express the interests of the wearer. The colors, fabrics, weaves, prints, and designs of scarves and neckties offer countless styles for collectors to choose from—and it's the variety of scarves and neckties which make them great collectibles.

There are many categories of scarves and neckties to choose from. Distinct patterns such as paisley, plaid, floral, or geometric designs vary so much by manufacturer that you could specialize in one of these, or you can select a specific subject.

Scarves or ties featuring cartoon characters, movie stars, or historical personalities are great areas to specialize in. There are even souvenir scarves and neckties printed with Seattle's Space Needle, New York City's Statue of Liberty, South Dakota's Mount Rushmore, and other tourist attractions. The logos or seals of universities, museums, cities, states, and countries can also be part of the design. Special interests such as flags, stamps, currency, and other items are also popular designs.

Some collectors specialize in the most tacky ties and scarves, while others seek beauty. Delicate embroidery, gold weaves, smooth silk, or hand painted, are elegant examples of the best neckties and scarves. Look at many different scarves or ties before you decide what to collect, and then begin your search.

Both scarves and neckties are sold in department, specialty, and gift stores. But, the problem with buying them new, is that they can cost anywhere from $10 to over $100. It's perhaps a better idea to begin your collection with used accessories.

Garage sales, flea markets, church bazaars, estate sales, thrift stores and auctions are good sources for used scarves and neckties. Depending upon the design and condition, prices can range from fifty cents to five dollars or more. Unless you're looking at very old clothing, even a good price guide won't help you. A general rule of thumb is that good used clothing should be priced anywhere between 5% and 15% of the original retail price. For this reason, it's a good idea to become familiar with department store prices.

If you can't wear each tie or scarf in your collection, try displaying some of them in your room. Drape scarves and ties over furniture, hang them on curtain rods, tie them around the necks of stuffed toys, or simply fold and lay them on a shelf to be admired. Be creative in how you show off your collection and it's sure to add a splash of color to your room.

At some point, you might even decide to use some of the fabric from your collection to make quilts, stuffed pillows, stuffed toys, or to upholster small objects. As long as the scarves or ties are not very old or valuable, this is a wonderfully practical use for your collection.

Collecting scarves or neckties can be both practical and fun. Look around and see what styles and designs you like, and then begin your search!

Related Collectibles: tie tacks, matching hats and gloves

81

Seashells

....

*"When you do dance,
I wish you
A wave o' the sea
that you might ever do
Nothing but that."*
William Shakespeare, 1564-1616

Seashells are masterpieces of nature and they come in an endless variety of designs. Tiny snail shells that are no bigger than a pencil eraser are swept to shore by rolling waves. The largest seashell, the Giant Clam can grow to more than five feet across resting on the ocean floor. Every color of the rainbow can be seen on seashells that wash ashore on warm tropical beaches. It's both the endless variety and intricate beauty of seashells that make them wonderful to collect.

There are over 75,000 different types of shells. Most of the large, colorful shells are home to marine animals that live in the ocean or saltwater marshes. Shells are also found in fresh water ponds, rivers, and lakes. Shells long abandoned by their inhabitants are embedded in rocks along river beds or left on sandy beaches.

The best way to collect shells is to find them yourself. Walking along the beach at low tide or after a major storm can yield many shells for your collection—and since gifts of nature are free, building a collection of found shells won't cost you a dime.

Although shells can be found in shallow tide pools, it's better to leave them in their watery homes undisturbed. The creatures that live in the shells may still be inside. Even when you find a shell on the beach, the tiny animal might still be inside the shell— so if you find that someone is at home, return the shell to the water and look for another one.

Seashells can smell very bad when you first take them home. Be sure to rinse them off in clean water and let them dry. If the shells still have an odor, soak them in a bowl of water with a few drops of liquid dish soap and then rinse again. After you've collected a few shells, you might want to find out what kind they are.

A good field guide, which can be found in the science or nature section of a local bookstore, should help you to identify your seashells. Field guides generally include pictures as well as size and distribution information. Study the field guide to learn what other kinds of shells are common in the area where you're collecting. If you have several examples of a particular type of shell, try trading with friends and other collectors.

If Channeled Whelks, Moon Shells, Razor Clams, Deep-Sea Scallops, Tortoiseshell Limpet, and other fascinating shells are not be plentiful where you live, you can still collect them. Even if you live a thousand miles away from an ocean beach, you can probably still find sea shells near you. Some retail stores carry seashells as either examples of nature or as decorator items. Among the best sand-free places to look for shells are at science or nature stores. These stores usually carry a wide variety of shells with prices starting at about $1. There are even gift and specialty stores that carry large, impressive shells. Unfortunately, these larger examples are much more expensive with prices ranging from $20 to over $200, depending upon the type, size, and condition of the shell.

Seashells make attractive displays in china cupboards, on bookshelves, or on table tops. If you have too many shells to display at once, you might try filling a fish bowl or other attractive clear glass container with the smaller shells so that some of them can be seen. You can rotate the larger shells so that most of your collection is displayed at one time or another.

Collecting seashells is a marvelous hobby. Hopefully, it will take you to the most beautiful lakes, rivers, and ocean beaches in the world. That in itself may be the greatest reward for collecting nature's gifts.

Related Collectibles: starfish, sharks teeth, rocks

SHEET MUSIC

"Sure there is music even in the beauty,
and the silent note which cupid strikes,
far sweeter than the sound of an instrument.
For there is a music wherever there is a harmony, order,
or proportion; and thus far we may maintain the music of the spheres."

Sir Thomas Browne, 1605-1682

Long before compact discs, personal stereos, or even radios, sheet music was printed so that musicians could correctly play and sing songs as they had been written. Beginning in the 1880s, sheet music became extremely popular. Opera houses, saloons, and musical theaters featured live entertainment. After the first movie theater opened up, piano players were soon hired to play background music for silent films. All of these live performances generated a growing need for sheet music—and it was published in great quantities. Today, sheet music is enjoyed by musicians and collectors alike.

There are at least two different kinds of sheet music collectors. Many musicians collect old sheet music to learn and preserve early ballads, hymns, jazz, or blues. Other collectors prize old sheet music not for the songs, but for the colorful lithographs printed on the front. One thing is certain, though—if you want a manageable sheet music collection, you have to specialize.

Collectors who want to preserve old music might have the easiest time deciding what kind of sheet music to specialize in. Many of these collectors choose the kind of sheet music they enjoy playing. Some possibilities include classical, blues, farm ballads, or the music of Broadway. For those collectors who are more interested in the cover art, deciding what to specialize in might be a bit more difficult.

Artistic lithographs were printed on the covers of most of the early sheet music. Some collectors specialize in sheet music with the faces of movie stars, sports heroes, or cartoon characters printed on the front. Katherine Hepburn, Babe Ruth, and Disney's Bambi are a few examples of the faces that you may find. Others look for sheet music with transportation themes such as airplanes, steamliners, or trains. Holiday, travel, or humorous covers are also interesting categories.

Old sheet music can be found at antique stores, paper shows, estate sales, and flea markets. The prices range from a few dollars to about $20, but most copies are valued at $5 or less. Try to become familiar with current sheet music values by getting a good price guide and talking with collectors and dealers. Once you have a pretty good idea of what you're looking for, and the prices you can expect to pay, you'll want to give some thought to storing and displaying your collection.

Sheet music can be kept in a photograph album, a scrapbook, stored in a cardboard box, or framed and hung on the wall. Framed sheet music will look good in almost any room in the house. If you use Plexiglas photograph frames with metal clips, you can easily rotate the sheet music on display.

Collecting old sheet music is a great way to preserve a bit of music history, while enjoying some wonderful lithographs. If you think you might enjoy collecting old sheet music, you aren't just whistling Dixie!

Related Collectibles: music books, records, tapes, compact discs

Small Appliances

....

"The Time Machine"
Title of a book by Herbert George Wells,
1866-1946

Perhaps the closest things we have to a time machine are the thousands of small appliances that have been produced since the Industrial Revolution. For almost every task, odd job, or project, man has invented a small appliance to make it easier. No better reflection of technology can be found than those portable pieces of everyday life. That's why small appliances, however funny it may seem, make great collectibles.

If necessity is the mother of invention as the saying goes, then convenience must be the father. Many different appliances have been introduced for our comfort and convenience. Fans, vacuums and sweepers, waffle irons, hand drills, apple peelers, and other appliances have evolved from rustic prototypes into the efficient, modern versions that we use today. With hundreds of different companies trying to "build a better mousetrap," the variety of designs for even a single appliance can be astonishing.

In fact, it can sometimes be difficult to tell exactly what an old appliance was used for. For example, the 1927 Sears, Roebuck and Company catalogue shows a round, vented cylinder with a center hand crank. Could this be a coffee grinder, an ice cream maker, or a pepper mill? No, it's an electric popcorn popper. Given the hot air and microwave models that we're familiar with today, very few of us could identify this small appliance correctly.

Some collectors specialize in a particular type of small appliance. Hand mixers, apple peelers, percolators, table fans, pencil sharpeners, and toasters are among the most collectible. Others collectors look for appliances from a particular era. The 1920s saw many new appliances introduced, which makes it a great decade for collectors.

It doesn't matter if the appliance is hand cranked or electric, as long as it's interesting. Old appliances suitable for collecting can be found at flea markets, garage sales, antique stores, auctions, and other secondhand sales. Prices range anywhere from a few dollars to well over $100, depending upon the type, age, manufacturer, and condition of the appliance.

Many collectors eventually learn how to repair the mechanical and electric parts of their appliances. This not only makes them usable, but it can also increase their value; however, make sure you have a parent or adult friend help with the repairs and testing. If you don't know what you're doing, this can be a dangerous endeavor.

Small appliances can be displayed on shelves or on tables. Displaying collectibles in the room which most matches their intended use, enhances the collection. For example, a collection of old toasters would look better in the kitchen than in the living room; however, if the only available space for the toaster collection is in the living room, then by all means, fill it up.

Collecting small appliances is a study of technology and innovation. It can be a lot of fun, too. If gadgets have always interested you, then small appliances might be the perfect collection!

Related Collectibles: machines, tools

Socks

....

"Now for good luck,
cast an old shoe after me."
John Heywood, ca. 1497-1580

There are many who think that lucky socks are preferable to getting an old shoe thrown at them. Today, hundreds of different designs have caused growing interest in socks as a favorite collectible. Before you laugh, consider the variety.

Designer socks with painted, printed, and embroidered patterns and pictures are almost as fashionable as neckties. Men, women, and children can slip their feet into argyle, paisley, geometric, and other interesting designs. Socks featuring clocks, flags, ducks, insects, and almost anything else you can think of are available on retailer shelves or in catalogues—and the subjects covered by sock designers run the gamut from advertising to politics.

For example, McDonalds, Nike, and other corporate logos have been featured on fuzzy footwear. A pair of smiling peanut socks touts President Carter as the candidate of choice. Socks printed with Disney and other cartoon characters can be found everywhere from the classroom to the boardroom. Socks with treads on the bottom, eyes on the top, and other variations bring a smile to our face and a bounce to our step.

Holiday socks are among the most popular collectible footwear. Christmas trees, presents, snowmen, Santa, reindeer, and other seasonal symbols grace our Yuletide socks. Pumpkins, bats, turkeys, flags, and bunnies are but a few of the

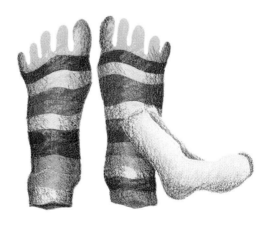

festive footwear, and with holiday socks, you can celebrate year-round. If this isn't enough variety, though, there are even more styles to consider.

Novelty socks fitted for individual toes, sewn with claws, or equipped with battery operated heaters can be found if you look hard enough. For more variety, take ordinary socks and create your own unique styles. Patches, glitter, sequins, buttons, and other accessories can personalize your sock collection even further—or consider foreign socks.

Socks made in other countries are sometimes unique enough to attract collectors. For example, socks that are made in Turkey are diamond-shaped and have no visible heal. The traditional designs of Turkish socks provide clues about the wearer's status—including whether or not the wearer is married. The patterns are bold and the colors are brilliant. Turkish socks, and probably other foreign-made socks might make an interesting collection by themselves.

Sock collectors usually display their prizes one pair at a time—while they're wearing them. They take great enjoyment in sharing them with others while keeping their toes warm. Mix and match or wear two of a kind—it's up to you. The important thing is to have a good time with this unique collectible.

Related Collectibles: tennis shoes, shoelaces

Space Collectibles

···

"Space, the final frontier.
These are the voyages of the Starship Enterprise.
Its five-year mission: to explore strange new worlds,
to seek out new life and new civilizations,
to boldly go where no man has gone before."

Introduction to the "Star Trek"
TV Series, 1966-1969

Few destinations capture the imagination as quickly as outerspace. From the first time we see the stars, we dream about traveling to distant galaxies. Almost all of us have imagined what it would be like to meet an alien from another planet—and even though we know better, many of us still look for the man on the moon. It's the beauty and mystery of both the known and the unknown that makes outerspace so intriguing and so collectible.

Space collectibles cover a broad range of things relating to the stars, planets, galaxies, aliens, and other intergalactic items. The options for collectors interested in this category are endless. Toys, movies, books, patches, pictures, and posters are but a few of the possibilities—but just like astronauts, space collectors have to know where they are going before take off.

Perhaps the best way to select an area to specialize in is to evaluate your interests. Do you like science fiction movies, eerie-looking aliens, and reruns of "The Jetsons?" If so, then maybe space collectibles from the imaginations of authors and artists would send you to the moon. Perhaps, though, you'd rather read about black holes, look at photographs of Mars, and chart the progress of the Space Shuttle? Well, if this sounds more like it, then you might enjoy a collection based on real science.

Space collectibles based on fiction probably outnumber those generated by real science. Television shows and movies such as *Buck Rogers*, *Star Trek*, *ET the Extra Terrestrial*, and *Star Wars* have given us an astonishing number of toys, plates, cups, holiday ornaments, and other collectibles. A visit to almost any department, toy, or gift store should produce several examples worth collecting. Also, consider science fiction books, video tapes, and any other creative space collectibles you might come across.

If you're more interested in collecting information, pictures, patches, and other items that are related to the study of outerspace, then begin your search at a book store. There are many great books on the stars, planets, space travel, and other areas which might be of interest. Next, look for a science or nature store at a nearby mall. Many of these stores have puzzles, games, charts, and even working telescopes for learning about everything from cosmic dust to galaxies. Finally, if you're able to, visit one of the Challenger Space Centers, NASA sites, or a planetarium. Usually, these centers are open to visitors and often have gift stores where realistic photographs, posters, models, patches, and other space collectibles are offered for sale.

If you think space collectibles are out of this world, then take off on a collecting adventure that's light years ahead of the rest!

Related Collectibles: other scientific collectibles

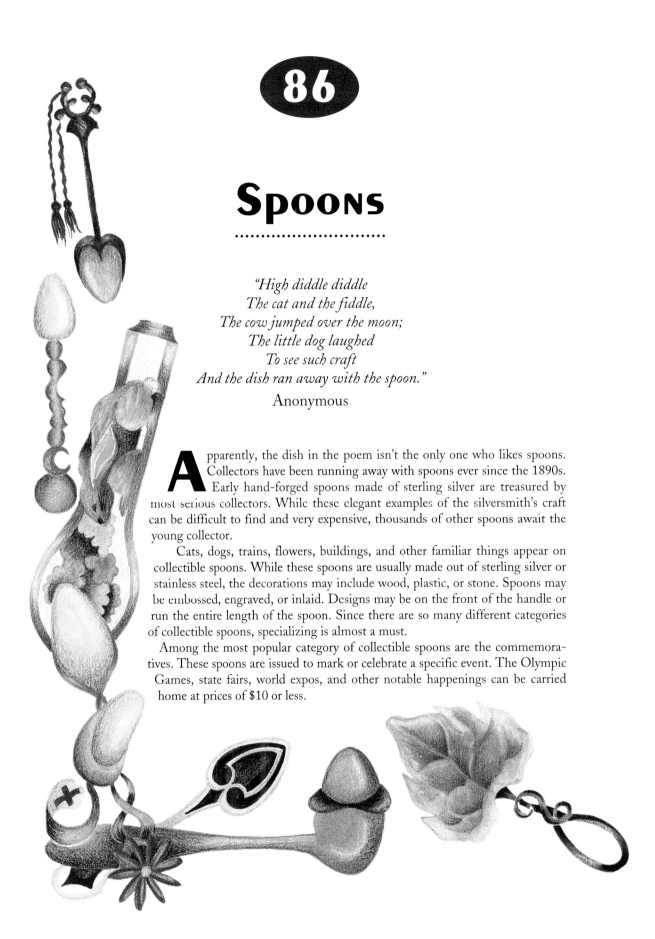

86

SPOONS

....

*"High diddle diddle
The cat and the fiddle,
The cow jumped over the moon;
The little dog laughed
To see such craft
And the dish ran away with the spoon."*

Anonymous

Apparently, the dish in the poem isn't the only one who likes spoons. Collectors have been running away with spoons ever since the 1890s. Early hand-forged spoons made of sterling silver are treasured by most serious collectors. While these elegant examples of the silversmith's craft can be difficult to find and very expensive, thousands of other spoons await the young collector.

Cats, dogs, trains, flowers, buildings, and other familiar things appear on collectible spoons. While these spoons are usually made out of sterling silver or stainless steel, the decorations may include wood, plastic, or stone. Spoons may be embossed, engraved, or inlaid. Designs may be on the front of the handle or run the entire length of the spoon. Since there are so many different categories of collectible spoons, specializing is almost a must.

Among the most popular category of collectible spoons are the commemoratives. These spoons are issued to mark or celebrate a specific event. The Olympic Games, state fairs, world expos, and other notable happenings can be carried home at prices of $10 or less.

Another related category is travel spoons. Almost everywhere you go, there's a wide variety of collectible spoons to choose from. For example, a Sequoia cactus is embossed on the handle of an Arizona spoon. An image of George Washington's Mt. Vernon reminds us of our first president and his Virginian plantation—and Oregon's state seal featured on a silver spoon makes a stately collectible. In fact, a great way to specialize might be to collect a spoon from every state.

How about collecting spoons from your favorite national parks? Yellowstone Park, The Everglades, Mount Rushmore, and other national parks are featured on a variety of spoons. If you are lucky enough to collect spoons during your travels, you might want to buy two of each kind—one for your collection and one to trade. Also, what about spoons with personality?

Character spoons are also quite popular, Little Red Riding Hood, Mary Poppins, Little Miss Muffet, Mickey Mouse and others sit atop collectible spoons. Famous personalities such as Abraham Lincoln, Benjamin Franklin, George Washington and other historical figures can also be found.

There are more categories to consider. Holiday, advertising, and religious are just a few of the possibilities. Think about what interests you the most, and then see if there are collectible spoons to match. Collect a certain type of spoon such as baby, iced tea, grapefruit, serving, or dessert spoons. Once you decide what kind of spoons to collect, then start looking.

Tourist, gift, and other specialty stores are about the best places to find new collectible spoons. Old or antique spoons are frequently sold at flea markets, antique shows, and auctions. The prices will depend on the design, age, subject, and what it's made of. Sterling silver is usually more expensive than either silver-plate or stainless steel. Keep in mind, though, that silver and silver plate spoons will need to be polished with a clean rag and silver cream.

For a traditional display, use a wooden rack which has been specially made for these spoons. Dealers who sell spoons can tell you where to find them—or you can set the spoons out on a shelf, keep them in a clear drinking glass, or even store them in a shoe box. Just make sure your collection is kept in a safe place where you can easily get to it.

The variety of subjects, ease of displaying, and affordability make spoons one of the best choices for young collectors. If you think spoons are neat, then dish yourself up a helping of fun by collecting them!

Related Collectibles: spoon rests, forks, cups, napkin rings

Sports Collectibles

*"[Baseball] breaks your heart.
It is designed to break your heart.
The game begins in the spring,
when everything else begins again, and it
blossoms in the summer,
filling the afternoons and evenings,
and then as soon as the chill rains come,
it stops, and leaves you to face the fall alone."*

A. Bartlett Giamattin, 1938-1989

Abner Doubleday is credited with giving us baseball in 1839. A game similar to modern football developed around 1869. Promoter John L. Sullivan popularized boxing in the 1880s, and basketball was invented in 1891, by Dr. James A. Naismith. Since these and other sports took root, collecting sports memorabilia has become a national pastime.

Everything from baseball cards to hunting decoys are collected by sports enthusiasts. The problem is not where to find these collectibles, but what to specialize in. The options for the sports enthusiast are almost unlimited. Without specializing, a collector could amass an unmanageable collection.

Almost every sport offers a tremendous amount and variety of collectibles. Team sports are well-represented with collectibles from high school, college, amateur, and professional teams. Football jerseys, baseball gloves, basketball pennants, soccer balls, and playbooks, are just a few of the possibilities. If you're lucky enough to attend live sporting events, then there are several "free" collecting opportunities.

Some collectors keep all of the ticket stubs from the games or matches they attend. The plastic drink cups with team logos are quite collectible, and the promotional items handed out on fan appreciation days are big crowd pleasers. On these special days, hats, miniature bats, balls, or other items are given away to the first several hundred in line. For those willing to pay a few extra dollars, official game programs also make great collectibles.

Non-team sports are also represented in the collecting frenzy. Some collectors look for hand-carved duck decoys, old skis and snowshoes, antique camping and hiking equipment, and all kinds of fishing gear. Also, old sports catalogues and books are highly sought after.

Sports collectibles are available almost everywhere. T-shirts, hats, bumper stickers, and other new sports collectibles can be found in grocery, department, gift, and sporting goods stores. Old or antique sports collectibles are sold at sports auctions, specialty shows, flea markets, and garage sales.

The prices for sports collectibles range anywhere from a few dollars to several thousand. The values are based on the kind of collectible, age, condition, and whether or not the item is signed by a well-known player. If you collect used or antique sports collectibles, get a good price guide to become familiar with current values.

There are a variety of ways to display sports collectibles. Items such as pennants, snowshoes and skis, tennis rackets, posters, golf clubs, and pictures are very attractive hanging on the wall. Hats, helmets, and baseball gloves can be displayed on coat trees or hat racks. Boxing gloves, decoys, bird calls, and balls display well on shelves. Finally, sports cards, photos, articles, magazines, and other paper collectibles are well-protected and easy to view in photograph albums.

Sports collectibles are almost as popular as the sports themselves. If you want to hit a home run with your collection, look for sports collectibles—they're a ball!

Related Collectibles: event collectibles, games

STAMPS

····························

*"He thought he saw an Albatross
That fluttered round the lamp:
He looked again, and found it was a
Penny postage stamp. 'You'd best be getting home,' he said,
The nights are very damp."*
Lewis Carroll, 1832-1898

The first postage stamp, issued in 1840, was a one penny stamp printed by Great Britain. A few years later, almost every developing country came out with their own stamp. The first stamp issued in the United States appeared in 1847, and not long after that, stamp collectors were enjoying their new hobby. Today, stamp collecting remains one of the most popular hobbies in the world, attracting collectors of all ages.

Perhaps the best way to begin collecting stamps is to start tearing them off of envelopes that arrive in the mail; however, make sure that you ask your parents first. The reason this is a great way to begin is that it will cost you absolutely nothing. While the stamps you collect from delivered mail will have cancellation marks, and probably won't go up much in value, they can get a young collector off to a good start.

Another way to begin collecting is to frequently visit your local post office to see what new stamps have come in. For example, in 1996, there were several new stamps issued due to the rise in postage rates. Cartoon characters, plants, country scenes, and many famous people made appearances on stamps during the year.

Some collectors specialize in a particular area of stamps. Animals, plants, architecture, and transportation are popular. Commemorative stamps marking events such as the first man on the moon, the Smithsonian's 150th Anniversary, or the Olympic Games, are also quite popular. Stamps with the faces of historical figures, movie stars, athletes, and musicians sometimes appeal to "non-collectors," simply because of their interest in the subject depicted on the stamp. While the United States can only feature the images of people who have died, many foreign governments print stamps with only the most popular personalities, whether they are living or not.

Many of today's celebrities are featured on the brightly colored stamps of Switzerland, Brazil, France, and other countries. Stamps issued by countries that no longer exist (such as the Soviet Union and

West Germany) are highly sought after. Also, when there's a change in a country's leadership, the stamps of that nation often reflect the transfer of power. In the Middle East, when the Shaw of Iran left power, stamps featuring his face all but disappeared and became quite collectible.

Among the most valuable stamps are limited editions or those featuring variations or mistakes. The most famous example of this is a U.S. Airmail stamp with an airplane printed upside-down. A more recent example, issued in the mid-1990s, was the snowman stamp printed with varying numbers of snowflakes. While these rarities are difficult to find, thousands of other collectible stamps are waiting to be discovered.

New issues are the easiest types of stamps to collect. The U.S. Post Office sells a wide variety of domestic stamps. There are also several mail order companies that offer foreign stamps. Early issues or canceled stamps are sometimes sold at auctions, antique stores, and at coin and stamp shops. Prices range from a few cents to several thousands of dollars. Before buying early issues or foreign stamps, get a good price guide to become familiar with current values. Call your post office to see if there's a local collector's group to join. Learning from other collectors is the best way to get started.

While stamps are typically kept in special albums or notebooks, they can also be stored in shoe boxes, tins, envelopes, or other containers. The important thing to remember is that stamps must stay dry. If they become damp, they may stick together and get ruined.

Collecting stamps is fun and it can reflect your interests. If you're stuck on stamps, then start collecting today!

Related Collectibles: Christmas and Easter Seals

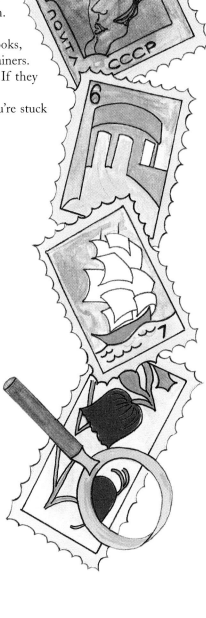

STATE and NATIONAL Collectibles

"Literature transmits incontrovertible
condensed experience . . .
From generation to generation.
In this way literature becomes the living memory
of a nation."

Alexander Isayevich Solzhenitsyn, 1918-

Remembering places where you've visited can open the door to a great collection. State and national collectibles come in all shapes, sizes, colors, and materials. It's almost guaranteed that your state and national collectibles will be one of the most unique collections on the block. Why? It's because with state and national collectibles, anything's possible!

If the quote above is correct, then literature is a wonderful collectible. Why not collect poetry from Oregon, Texas, Virginia, or the state where you live? What about romance, mystery, science fiction, or any other genre that interests you from the state or states of your choice? Does the work of English playwrights speak to you? Look for British plays to build a national collection of writing.

How about collecting something a little more tasty? Every state and nation is known for one or more culinary specialties. A collection of these tantalizing recipes would make an interesting collection. For example, Texas is known for chili, Pennsylvania is famous for sauerkraut, and Louisiana is gumbo country. Like states, countries also have special foods.

The United States dishes up great apple pie, Mexico serves a variety of enchiladas, and fish and chips are on virtually all menus in England. There are many different recipes for each dish. Any recipe that reminds you of a particular state or country is fair game for your collection. Once collected, the best way to share a recipe collection is to prepare some of the dishes.

How about a state or national trivia collection? Find out what the state birds are for each state and "capture" them with your camera. How about a state flower, rock, insect, or animal collection? Any of these would make an interesting state collection. Collect your way through boutiques, stores, and shops as you travel.

T-shirts, mugs, plates, pencils, and other collectibles are printed with the name, official seal, or scenic views of almost every state and country on the planet, and the outline of many states and countries are the inspiration for cake pans, serving bowls, decorative figures, and other souvenir items. Perhaps one of the most fun state or country-shaped collectibles are cookie cutters. A collection of 50 state-shaped cookie cutters would indeed make an impressive display! These types of collectibles are often found in gift shops, specialty stores, and any areas where tourists can be found. Naturally, the best assortment of collectibles are found in their home state or country, but there are other possibilities as well.

Garage sales, flea markets, church bazaars, and auctions are among the best places to find state and national items. The prices of these secondhand collectibles are usually only a fraction of their retail price.

Building a collection of state and national collectibles is a lot of fun. It's one collection that will keep you going places!

Related Collectibles: geographic collectibles

90

Stereo and Three-Dimensional Viewers

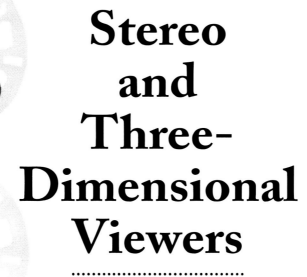

....

"I want to reach that state of condensation of sensations which constitutes a picture."
Henri Matisse, 1869-1954

Viewing majestic mountains, city scapes, or magnificent animals in three dimensional or stereo photographs is the "next best thing to being there." Look at a stereo picture through a viewer and see if you can resist reaching out to touch something in the picture to see if it's real.

A pair of photographs taken from slightly different viewpoints, create the three-dimensional effect. The depth and detail of these pictures have collectors snapping them up faster than you can say "cheese."

Since 1850, millions of stereo pictures had been taken by professional and amateur photographers. By the 1890s, almost every parlor in the United States was furnished with a stereo viewer and an assortment of views. Stereo viewers were the television of their time, entertaining families and their guests throughout the evening.

The variety of three-dimensional subjects is mind boggling. Take a trip to the muddy streets of Victorian Webster City, Iowa, the English Church in Jerusalem, Palestine, the lofty solitude of the Swiss Alps, and other exotic and interesting places without leaving the comfort of your living room. All you need is a vintage viewer to go along with the views.

The most popular antique viewers, called stereoscopes, date from the 1870s and look similar to a pair of binoculars. The most visible difference between the viewer and a pair of binoculars is the sliding card holder. Twin photographs are printed on stiff cards and placed in the holder for viewing. Prices for viewers range from $25 to over $200, depending upon the age, manufacturer, condition, and what they're made of. The cards are much more affordable, with prices ranging from a few dollars to around $50 a piece, but if you want something more recent, new stereo viewers and pictures are plentiful.

Although there are a few different modern viewers, the most widely known are ViewMasters. The ViewMaster is a binocular-shaped viewer which holds a round reel containing seven pairs of pictures. By pulling a lever on the side of the viewer, the reel turns and changes the picture. Modern ViewMaster viewers cost anywhere from $5 for a brand new viewer up to $50 for an early model—and there are a variety of reels to choose from.

Modern ViewMaster reels cover a variety of subjects including travel, entertainment, and industry. This is just a fraction of the possibilities, though. There are many other categories waiting to be discovered, but since no one can collect them all, you might want to specialize.

Advertising, television shows, movies, cartoons, parks, caves, transportation, people, or views of a particular city or state are all good starting points. It's only the starting point, because a collector's interest often grows into several areas of related subjects. For example, a collector who specializes in circus views might expand into carnivals, expos, fairs, and other entertainment events. Prices for new or used ViewMaster reels range from $3 to over $50 per three-reel set.

Stereo viewers, view cards, and reels are sold at antique shows, auctions, and at flea markets. New viewers and reels can also be found at toy, discount, and gift stores.

Collecting stereo views and viewers is great fun—and, for many, they're a picture-perfect collectible!

Related Collectibles: photographs, camera equipment

91

Stuffed Toys

"The gingham dog went 'Bow-wow-wow!'
And the Calico Cat replied 'Mee-ow!'
The air was littered an hour or so,
With bits of gingham and calico."

Eugene Field, 1850-1895

It was a fabled day in 1926, when Christopher Robin's stuffed toys came to life in A.A. Milne's Winnie-the-Pooh stories. Greedy Pooh Bear, timid Piglet, melancholy Eeyore, irrepressible Tigger, and Kanga and Baby Roo are known and loved by many—and they are in good company.

Ever since the first piece of fabric was wrapped around a wad of straw, children have loved stuffed toys. Bears, elephants, monkeys, dogs, cats, and even insects are endearing when they're soft, stuffed, and sewn. Who doesn't have a favorite stuffed toy or two? They are the fuzzy little creatures that inhabit our shelves, beds, and bedrooms, and they're one of the most popular collectibles of all times.

Many who collect stuffed toys don't even realize that they do. Perhaps you're even one of them. Look in your room, the family room, and anywhere else you keep your things, and count the number of stuffed toys. If your tally is more than one dozen, you're probably a collector! The good news is there are many more stuffed toys waiting to be collected.

Stuffed toys are like rabbits—they tend to multiply. For this reason, many collectors specialize. Collect dogs, cats, clowns, dolls, penguins, or any of your other favorites. Look for antiques, new, or used playthings and discover an amazing variety of stuffed toys.

Antique stuffed toys include Margaret Steiff's early creations, teddy bears, Raggedy Ann and Andy dolls, and various handmade stuffed toys from all over the world. These fine examples of early craftsmanship are among the most expensive stuffed toys, with prices exceeding $2,000. For this reason, most young collectors look for new or used toys.

Stuffed toys can be found at toy, gift, discount, specialty, and almost any other type of retail outlet. Prices for these familiar friends range from one dollar to well over $200. The good news is that stuffed toys are some of the most frequently sold and least expensive garage sale items.

The kids next door, the teacher across the street, and even the retired couple down the lane probably have stuffed toys that are no longer wanted. They may sell them at garage sales, donate them to a church bazaar, or give them away. If you're lucky, you might be the one to carry them home. All you have to do is look, listen, and ask if anyone has stuffed toys for your collection. When you find stuffed toys at secondhand sales, the prices should range from a few cents up to a few dollars. Keep in mind that used stuffed toys usually require a little work.

Read the label, and if it's machine washable, make sure to wash each toy in warm water and detergent. Inspect all toys before and after washing to see if any minor repairs are necessary.

Stuffed toys are nicely displayed on shelves, beds, sofas, or hanging in a toy hammock in the corner of your room. Collecting stuffed toys is a fun and inexpensive way to keep some fury friends close at hand. Round up some of these adorable creatures, and start collecting stuffed toys today!

Related Collectibles: toys, dolls

T-shirts

· ·

*"My parents went to Hawaii
and all I got was this lousy T-shirt!"*
Anonymous on T-shirt

In 1942, the United States Navy introduced a knitted, cotton undershirt with short sleeves and a round collar. Called "Ts" because they were shaped like a "T" when laid flat, the shirts became popular in 1955, when actor James Dean, wore one in the movie, *Rebel Without a Cause*. Today, wearing a T-shirt can be a political, fashion or interest statement. Or, it can be a great way for a collector to show off their collection.

Many people who collect T-shirts don't even realize they do. Go look in your closet. You might even be one of these unknowing collectors. Almost without trying, a mountain of T-shirts can pile up on your closet shelf. Before you know it, a collection large enough to rival a department store's stock, has taken root.

Most people buy T-shirts for themselves, receive them as gifts, or win them. Often, they are given away at local sporting events, to winners of radio station contests, or as promotional items. At prices of $5 to $30, or as little as $1 for used shirts, they are very affordable. With thousands and thousands of different designs, T-shirts make great collectibles.

Many collectors specialize in a particular subject. Sports, travel, humor, and politics are among the most common T-shirt topics. Do you have a favorite baseball, football, or basketball team? Then you can collect T-shirts bearing your team's logo. If you or your family travels, then how about collecting a T-shirt from everywhere you vacation? If you're a fan of Gary Larson, Charles Schultz, or knock, knock jokes, then building a collection of funny shirts might be a lot of laughs. If you're interested in politics, why not collect T-shirts with the faces, slogans, or symbols of politicians and their parties?

Some collectors really work hard to build their collections. They only collect shirts they've earned by running a race, playing a team sport, participating in a charity event, or by winning a contest. These are, perhaps, the most prized T-shirts because of the effort that was put in to getting them. If you would rather let someone else make the effort, though, then advertising shirts might be ideal.

Advertising T-shirts are both sold and given away. Some collectors only look for free T-shirts, while others are willing to pay a nominal fee and a few box tops to have a Mr. Bubble, 7-UP, or an Oreo T-shirt. These shirts can be a lot of fun to collect, particularly if the product's package design or logo changes over time.

Another popular topic for T-shirt collectors is animals. Cats, birds, fish, monkeys, elephants, seals, whales, and other animals are printed on T-shirts. These shirts are often very colorful with designs on the front, back, and even on the sleeves. You can focus your collecting even more by looking for shirts with a certain type of animal on it—panda bears, for example. The options for T-shirt collectors are almost unlimited.

While T-shirts are sold in almost any retail store, they can also be found at very low prices at secondhand sales. Since T-shirts have a way of accumulating quickly, you can almost always count on finding them at garage sales, flea markets, and church bazaars. Take advantage of bargain prices when you can, and your collection will grow rapidly.

T-shirts can be nicely displayed on hangers, framed in Plexiglas, or even tacked up on your wall (with your parents' permission); however, most collectors take great pleasure in wearing the shirts in their collection.

Collecting T-shirts can be a lot of fun, and will always leave you with more than just the shirt on your back.

Related Collectibles: Hawaiian shirts, baseball caps

93

TelepHone InsulAtors

*"Once there was an elephant
Who tried to use the telephant –
No! No! I mean an elephone
Who tried to use the telephone."*
Laura Elizabeth Richards, 1850-1943

With the invention of the telegraph in 1844, insulators were developed to hold the electrical transmission wires to the poles. When Alexander Graham Bell gave us the telephone in 1876, the use of insulators became even more widespread. Known today as telephone insulators, these antiquated devices are now one of the earliest technology collectibles.

There are more than 3,000 different types of telephone insulators known to exist. Manufactured in a variety of styles and colors, there are glass, pottery, and wooden examples. Threadless insulators, which were made between 1850 and 1865, were used in the days of the telegraph. These insulators are often expensive and difficult to find; however, more recent examples can be found for as little as a few dollars.

Many telephone insulators were embossed with the patent dates, which provide clues to their values. The value of an insulator depends upon the age, color, and condition. As a general rule, the oldest insulators are the most expensive; however, if a common early example has cracks or chips, then it might sell for less than $50. The color also influences the value of insulators. For example, aqua and green glass are among the most common, making them less valuable. Colors such as light or ice blue, clear, and black are highly prized. Carnival glass insulators are highly collectible, too. While it's rumored that red glass insulators once were made, none are known to exist today; however, if a genuine red insulator did turn up, it would command a high price.

Affordable telephone insulators can be found at antique shops, flea markets, and at auctions; however, it's a good idea to get a price guide to become familiar with the manufacturers, styles, and values. Also, it's likely there are at least a few antique dealers near you who are willing to share information.

Telephone insulators make great shelf displays in almost any room of the house. They work well as bookends, paperweights, and decoration.

Collecting insulators is like keeping a bit of history right in your very own home—and, it can be a lot of fun!

Related Collectibles: telephone collectibles, lightning rod balls

94

Thimbles

....

"They sought it with thimbles, they sought it with care;
They pursued it with forks and hope;
They threatened its life with a railway share;
They charmed it with smiles and soap."
Lewis Carroll, 1832-1898

Long before sewing machines were invented, mending garments was done by hand. Seamstresses the world over could testify to the importance of a good thimble for doing needlework. All it takes is one needle prick to fully appreciate them for their intended use; however, it takes a little closer inspection to see their history, beauty and variety. Be forewarned, though. If you take a close look at these little finger caps, you might just end up collecting them.

There are over 1,000 different types of thimbles made out of wood, plastic, glass, porcelain, bone, brass, pewter, silver, gold, and other metals. Thimbles have been cast, carved, hand-painted, and decaled to create an amazing variety of beautiful, yet useful sewing tools. There are fancy thimbles, which were once used at sewing socials in fine parlors, and plain thimbles for everyday needlework. It's the fancy thimbles of the nineteenth century, though, which attract the most interest from collectors.

Early thimbles come in a variety of designs. Turtles, scrolls, flowers, cherubs, initials, towers, and other decorations are treasured by thimble collectors. Elaborate Victorian figural, commemorative, and advertising thimbles are also quite collectible—and when women were granted the right to vote in 1920, many politicians gave away campaign thimbles to win the feminine vote.

Antique thimbles are not only scarce, they can also be expensive. For this reason, you might want to begin by collecting new thimbles.

Limited edition silver and porcelain thimbles, made especially for the collectibles market, are being manufactured all over the world. These delightful finger caps can be found in department and specialty stores and through mail-order. The prices for reproductions depend upon the material, design, and the detail of each thimble; however, you should note that some of these reproduction thimbles show up at antique shops, flea markets, and auctions priced at many times their actual value. Some unknowing or unscrupulous dealers are selling them as antiques. Before buying an "antique" thimble, you should get a good reference guide and become familiar with the styles, manufacturer's marks, and values.

Another type of collectible thimble is modern state thimbles. In almost every shop that's selling state souvenirs, you can find porcelain thimbles with the name, seal, or a tiny scenic view of the state on it. A collection containing all 50 states would make a wonderful display.

Probably the best way to display thimbles is to set them inside either a shadow box or a printer's tray. Both of these hanging frames have tiny shelves that would accommodate a collection of thimbles, and a hanging display of thimbles can be as artistically appealing as a fine painting.

Collecting thimbles is a time-honored tradition with as much variety as any collector could hope for. If you're a seamstress at heart, then consider collecting thimbles, and you'll have a great collection sewn up in no time!

Related Collectibles: needlework boxes, tape measures, and other sewing items

95

Tools

....

"Every tool carries with it the spirit by which it has been created."

Werner Karl Heisenberg, 1901-1976

The earliest hammer was probably a hand-held rock, used to chip stones into useful shapes. Other oddly-shaped stones remain as evidence that prehistoric man crafted and used tools. Axes, chisels, and grinding stones were made for specific tasks when the need arose. Even in the early years of the United States, tools were still being handmade by those who needed them. In fact, it wasn't until after the Civil War that manufacturers sprung up and began mass producing tools. These mass-produced tools are the kind that most collectors will find.

Collecting tools is a very interesting hobby. Because of the advances in technology over the past 100 years, some tools have changed drastically while others have become totally obsolete. It's the variety of both design and purpose that makes collecting tools so much fun!

A good reference and price guide covering the use, age, and value of old tools should be your first purchase. Before beginning the search, you should decide what kind of tools you want to collect.

The choices for tool collectors are many. Do you want to specialize in a particular kind of tool? There are wrenches, saws, tongs, levels, hand drills, clamps, and many other tools to consider. Even among these seemingly single-purpose tools, there's a great deal of diversity. For example, if you like hammers, how about ball pein, nail, ripping, riveting, or sledge hammer to name a few? All of these hammers vary in appearance and are uniquely suited for a specific purpose.

Another favorite collectible is the wood plane. These early wood shaving tools come in a variety of sizes, shapes, and styles. Block, grooving, circular, bull-nose rabbet, and beading planes are just a few examples of the styles which can be collected. While the old wooden planes are the most popular, metal planes are also highly collectible—as well as tools from the hands of skilled tradesmen.

Woodworkers, blacksmiths, machinists, plumbers, watchmakers, masons, lumbermen, glaziers, and other professionals carry boxes full of specialty tools. If you're still not sure what to collect, though, then how about obsolete tools? Among the most interesting tools are those that technology has left behind.

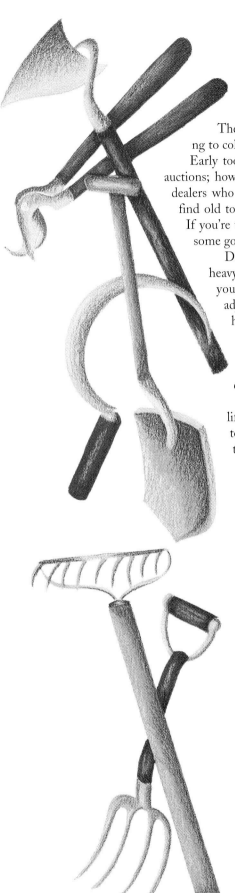

When the automobile replaced wagons and buggies, many of the tools which were used to repair these horse-drawn vehicles faded into history. For example, wheel wrenches, spoke pointers, and shaves, can no longer be found in hardware stores or catalogues. These tools would be especially interesting for those wanting to collect a little piece of history.

Early tools are often found at antique shops, flea markets, and auctions; however, they can be very expensive when purchased from dealers who specialize in them. For this reason, the best places to find old tools are garage sales, farm auctions, and church bazaars. If you're willing to look, and have a bit of luck, you should find some good buys.

Displaying old tools can be tricky. Some tools are very heavy or sharp, so it's a good idea to have a grown-up help you create your display. A new piece of pegboard with adjustable hooks will work very well to display wrenches, hammers, or saws. Wood planes, levels, and other bulky tools display better on shelves. Regardless of how you display your tools, make sure they're safe from small children or pets who might play with or knock them down.

Tools are an interesting collectible that can provide a lifetime of enjoyment. Most of them can be really useful tools—so set your sights on man's ingenuity, and collect tools!

Related Collectibles: hardware, small appliances

96

Tops

*"Hither and thither spins
The windborne, mirroring soul;
A thousand glimpses wins,
And never sees a whole."*

Matthew Arnold, 1822-1888

Spinning tops are one of the oldest known toys in the world. These whirling, twirling, colorful saucers can be found in almost every toy box. Although tops have entertained children for centuries, their popularity among collectors is fairly recent. Big ones, little ones, and every size in between, make collecting tops a great adventure.

Over the years, tops have been fashioned out of wood, stone, metal, and plastic. Early tops were painted vibrant colors or decorated with colorful lithography. Modern tops, often encase decorative pictures or figures under protective plastic domes. The variety of styles and subjects lead many collectors to specialize.

Tops made in the 1960s, have tin bodies and wooden handles. These lithographed gems are elaborately decorated with toy soldiers, bears, trains, dolls, and other fun things. These metal tops, which were made in a variety of designs, are among the most collectible.

Tops decorated with wagons, trains, boats, and even airplanes are collected by those interested in transportation. Clowns, lions, jugglers, big top tents, and trapeze artists attract circus collectors, and animals, cartoon characters, and other toys have taken a few spins on tops.

Among the most collectible tops are those with recognizable cartoon characters. Mickey Mouse, Yogi Bear, Bugs Bunny, and other animated friends can be found on both foreign and domestic tops. The presence of any of these lovable characters on a top means that the competition to find them will be stiff. Animation collectors are always interested in toys, plates, or anything else with the faces of their favorite characters on it; therefore, the prices for cartoon character tops may be expensive. If you see an affordable top with Woody Woodpecker, Mighty Mouse, Fred Flintstone, or any other cartoon character on it, buy it!

A variety of old advertising and political tops are also quite collectible. Banks, bakeries, car dealerships, and other businesses used to give away promotional tops. The hope was that every time the top was played with, the parents would think favorably on the business that provided it. Presidential-hopeful William McKinley asked Gibbs Manufacturing Company to make tops with the slogans "McKinley on Top" and "I Spin For McKinley," printed on them. In 1896, McKinley, and his tops, spun through a tough election to become President of the United States.

If these early tops are either too difficult to find or too expensive, then consider new tops. Even in this age of high-tech toys, tops are still spinning off the assembly line. Plastic tops with modern whirling action and contemporary designs are released each year. Look for new tops in toy stores, gift shops, and specialty stores.

Some of the new tops even combine new technology with their simple approach to fun. There are tops that whistle, spark, light up, and rattle as they spin. Any of these special effects make them particularly interesting to collectors.

Collecting tops is like a good game of hide-and-seek. It might take a bit of looking but the reward in the end is worth it. If you like these twirling toys and are up for the challenge, take some tops out for a spin.

Related Collectibles: yo-yos and other spinning toys

97

TRANSPORTATION Collectibles

···

"The white sails still fly seaward, seaward flying
Unbroken wings.
And the lost heart stiffens and rejoices
In the lost lilac and the lost sea voices
And the weak spirit quickens to rebel
For the bent goldenrod and the lost sea smell."

Thomas Stearns Eliot, 1888-1965

To some, the greatest sounds in the world are train whistles, jet engines, and the flap of sails. These are the dreamers, wanderers, or adventurers who yearn to travel to foreign ports, breathe the air of exotic islands, and drink the pure water of unknown springs. Perhaps, these are even the same people who seek transportation collectibles.

Transportation collectibles cover a wide variety of subjects. Virtually every type of vehicle that floats, flys, or runs on wheels is a target for collectors. Passenger ships, railroads, airplanes, and automobiles are at the top of this expansive category.

The first seafaring vessel was built around 8000 B.C. in the eastern Mediterranean. Ever since that maiden voyage, the ocean and the ships that have sailed her, have captured the dreams of many would-be sailors. The adventure and romance of the high seas has caused interest in passenger ship collectibles to swell. Menus, baggage labels, deck plans, and brochures are among the most affordable passenger ship collectibles. If you're a landlubber, then trains might be more on track.

Steam trains came into service in the 1830s, carrying economic and social change with them. Over 170 different railroad lines crisscrossed the United States bringing a variety of future collectibles. Today, demand for railroad collectibles exceeds the supply, making most of the older railroad related items quite expensive; however, if you are willing to look, you can probably find playing cards, linens, and glassware for less than $20. Some collectors specialize in a particular railroad line, while others try to collect something from each line that existed. For collectors whose dreams soar to loftier heights, airplane collectibles really take off.

Ever since Orville and Wilbur Wright made their historic fifty-seven second flight in 1903, man has been enchanted with air travel. It's no wonder, then, that airline collectibles attract so many collectors. Decks of cards, children's badges, coloring books, and other promotional give-a-ways are highly sought after. Silverware, china, and other marked service items are also popular. If public transportation takes a back seat to cars, then start up your engines, because automobile collectibles are plentiful.

Old car collectibles include manuals, catalogues, hood ornaments, early license plates, steering wheels, spark plugs, or just about any part that can be found at junk yards or antique auto parts shows. New collectibles include key chains, dealer tags, manuals, patches, and many other items which can be found in automotive, discount, or gift stores.

Transportation collectibles have been prized by collectors for many years. If you want a collection that will really take you places, transportation collectibles might just be the ticket!

Related Collectibles: transportation toys

98

TRANSPORTATION
Toys

·················

"When I was a beggarly boy,
And lived in a cellar damp,
I had not a friend nor a toy,
But I had Aladdin's lamp."

James Russell Lowell, 1819-1891

Even with Aladdin's lamp, it would be difficult to conjure up a more impressive area of collecting than transportation toys. Wagons, bicycles, cars, planes, trains, zephyrs, and countless other modes of transportation have been miniaturized as toys. It's no wonder, then, that the transportation toy is the most popular category of toy collecting on the planet.

From the antique tin vehicles of the 1700s, to the Hot Wheels of the 1990s, transportation toys are nothing but fun. And with a countless number of manufacturers and individual craftspeople making transportation toys, collecting has never been better.

Most collectors focus on a specific type of toy or build a collection based upon what the toys are made of. For example, a collection of trains might include toys dating from the 1800s through the 1990s—or the collection might only include trains made out of wood, tin, or cast iron. The availability and cost of any transportation toy depends upon the age, material, and the manufacturer.

Naturally, antique or older toys tend to be more expensive, and they can be difficult to find. For this reason, a collector just starting out might want to collect new transportation toys. Even if you restrict your collecting to new toys, the variety is great!

Electric trains, battery operated airplanes, and friction cars line the toy store isles. Rugged plastic jeeps, carved wooden trucks, and balsa wood rockets are yours to collect. Depending upon what you specialize in, you can expect to pay anywhere from $5 and up. If you want to join thousands of today's collectors who spend about $1 per toy, though, then look at Matchbox, Hot Wheels, and other die-cast vehicles.

Matchbox miniatures were introduced in 1953 with a larger, more detailed series of vehicles following in 1957. Today, it's estimated that about 75 million Matchbox cars roll off the assembly line each year. This tiny traffic jam includes almost every kind of road vehicle. Chevys, Jaguars, Jeeps, Fords, Land Rovers, Dodges, and other popular makes are parked in sandboxes everywhere. Even tot-sized utility vehicles such as road rollers, cement mixers, tankers, tractors, and cranes can be found. Motorcycles, hovercrafts, seafire boats, and countless others offer even more variety.

If you feel the need for speed, though, then check out Hot Wheels. Hot Wheels first zoomed off the shelves in 1968. These toys were not only flashy with their custom paint and decals, but they were also the fastest cars on the kitchen floor. Fantasy vehicles, hot rods, muscle cars, racers, and trucks are at the forefront of the Hot Wheels line. As with Matchbox toys, most new Hot Wheels can be purchased for around $1. Although these are two of the most popular types of die-cast toys, there are many other brands.

In fact, die-cast vehicles have become so popular that many limited editions are released each year. These are typically priced a bit higher cost $10 or more.

Collecting transportation toys, whether new or antique, is great fun. You can learn about different makes of vehicles, modes of transportation, and build a great collection in the process. If transportation toys rev up your engine, zoom out to a toy store and start collecting!

Related Collectibles: transportation collectibles

99

TRIVETS

············

"Right as a trivet."
Charles Dickens, 1812-1870

While trivets may not be the hottest collectible in the world, they were designed to withstand the heat. Originally, trivets were a household necessity. Hot kettles and irons heated on the coal stove or kitchen range, were placed on trivets to protect the table below. Today, while they're primarily a decorative accessory, trivets are also becoming a popular collectible.

Early trivets were made out of wrought iron, brass, and cast iron. Popular designs dating back to the late 1800s include portraits of famous people, animals, flowers, and fruit. While some of these examples of early American craftsmanship can be found at antique sales, auctions, and flea markets, they are becoming increasingly difficult to find. With prices for antique trivets ranging from $50 and up, young collectors might want to begin by collecting new trivets.

Trivets can be found in almost any grocery, department, discount, or gift store. Grocery stores carry either very simple designs or those reflecting local interests such as a university, tourist attraction, or the city itself. Highly polished brass, silver, and gold-plated trivets are frequently available at the fine department stores. The greatest variety of trivets are available in small gift or specialty stores.

Wood, stone, wicker, brass, iron, and tiles are among the most common materials used for new trivets. Designs are carved, stamped, decaled, painted, or drawn. Used primarily for decorative purposes today, trivets cover a diverse range of subjects. The only question is where to begin?

Most collectors narrow the search by specializing in a particular type of trivet. You can either select a particular subject, or collect trivets made out of a certain kind of material.

Chickens, houses, cows, hearts, birds, flowers, and many other subjects are featured on modern trivets, and the subjects can differ depending upon where they're being sold. For example, in Texas, there are cactus, longhorn cattle, and cowboy hat trivets. In Virginia, pineapples, mountains, and Colonial designs are popular. If you know someone who travels, then collecting regional trivets with state seals or tourist attractions might be fun.

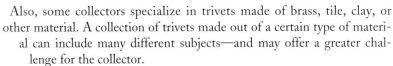

Also, some collectors specialize in trivets made of brass, tile, clay, or other material. A collection of trivets made out of a certain type of material can include many different subjects—and may offer a greater challenge for the collector.

New trivets can cost $5 or more, depending on the design, detail, and craftsmanship that went into making it. Be aware that there are many new trivets which are copies or reproductions of antiques. These trivets are becoming quite collectible themselves, and should be priced considerably less than their antique counterparts.

Trivets display well on tables, shelves, in china cupboards, or hanging on the wall. They are affordable, cover a variety of subjects, and can be a lot of fun to collect. So, for a collection that's "right as a trivet," start collecting trivets today!

Related Collectibles: kitchen collectibles, irons

100

WALKING STICKS AND FANCY CANES

"When Mrs. Frederick C. Little's second son was born,
everybody noticed that he was not much bigger than a mouse.
The truth of the matter was,
the baby looked very much like a mouse in every way. He
was only two inches high; and he had a mouse's sharp nose,
a mouse's tail, a mouse's whiskers, and the pleasant,
shy manner of a mouse.
Before he was many days old
he was not only looking like a mouse
but acting like one, too – wearing a gray hat
and carrying a small cane."
Elwyn Brooks White, 1899-1985

Hand-carved walking sticks and fancy canes have long been a sign of individual interests, tastes, and prominence. Today, they are attracting an increasing number of collectors who appreciate the beauty, skill, and genius that went into making them.

Hand-carved walking sticks are wonderful examples of folk art. Some of the older sticks which are often dated, have magnificent carvings of animals, birds, human faces, and other elaborate designs. While these old sticks are both difficult to find and expensive, new sticks can be found in great variety.

Carved walking sticks are sometimes sold at gift stores in state and national parks, craft shows, and at specialty stores. Many of these staffs were carved for hikers to lean on as they climbed up steep trails. These modern examples of the wood carver's craft are priced at $15 or more. The price will vary depending upon the type of wood and how detailed the carving is. If you enjoy a touch of elegance, though, perhaps you should collect fancy canes.

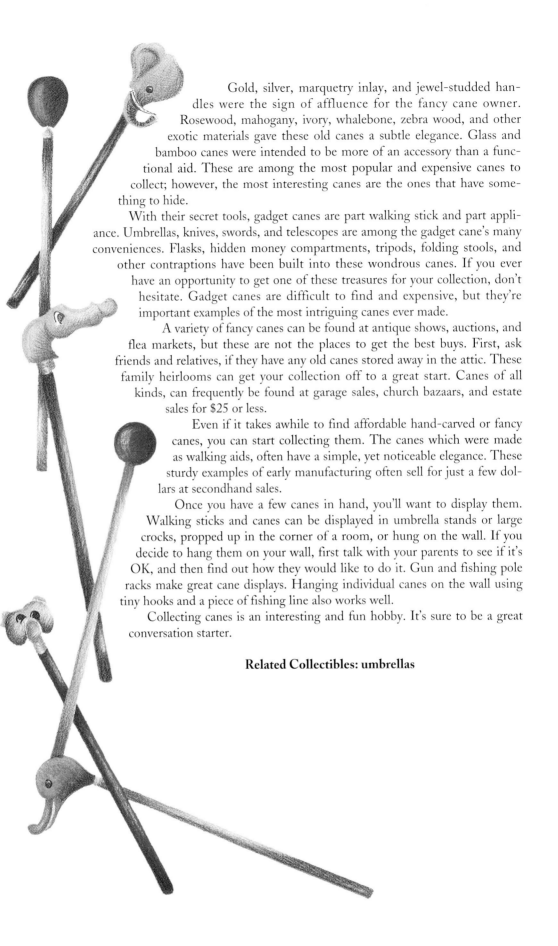

Gold, silver, marquetry inlay, and jewel-studded handles were the sign of affluence for the fancy cane owner. Rosewood, mahogany, ivory, whalebone, zebra wood, and other exotic materials gave these old canes a subtle elegance. Glass and bamboo canes were intended to be more of an accessory than a functional aid. These are among the most popular and expensive canes to collect; however, the most interesting canes are the ones that have something to hide.

With their secret tools, gadget canes are part walking stick and part appliance. Umbrellas, knives, swords, and telescopes are among the gadget cane's many conveniences. Flasks, hidden money compartments, tripods, folding stools, and other contraptions have been built into these wondrous canes. If you ever have an opportunity to get one of these treasures for your collection, don't hesitate. Gadget canes are difficult to find and expensive, but they're important examples of the most intriguing canes ever made.

A variety of fancy canes can be found at antique shows, auctions, and flea markets, but these are not the places to get the best buys. First, ask friends and relatives, if they have any old canes stored away in the attic. These family heirlooms can get your collection off to a great start. Canes of all kinds, can frequently be found at garage sales, church bazaars, and estate sales for $25 or less.

Even if it takes awhile to find affordable hand-carved or fancy canes, you can start collecting them. The canes which were made as walking aids, often have a simple, yet noticeable elegance. These sturdy examples of early manufacturing often sell for just a few dollars at secondhand sales.

Once you have a few canes in hand, you'll want to display them. Walking sticks and canes can be displayed in umbrella stands or large crocks, propped up in the corner of a room, or hung on the wall. If you decide to hang them on your wall, first talk with your parents to see if it's OK, and then find out how they would like to do it. Gun and fishing pole racks make great cane displays. Hanging individual canes on the wall using tiny hooks and a piece of fishing line also works well.

Collecting canes is an interesting and fun hobby. It's sure to be a great conversation starter.

Related Collectibles: umbrellas

101

Yo-Yos

··

"Look not thou down but up!"
Robert Browning, 1812-1889

Can you walk the dog, rock the baby, or go around the world? If the answers are a resounding "yes," then you've probably played with a yo-yo before. From the primeval jungles in the Philippines, to the schoolyard blacktops in the United States, yo-yos have mesmerized us with their spinning, whirling action. Today, many collectors are looking up, down, and all around for these popular toys.

Although it's believed that yo-yos got their start as a weapon in the Philippine jungles, the earliest recorded evidence that they existed, comes from ancient Greece. A vase from about 500 B.C. shows a picture of a boy playing with a toy that's similar to today's yo-yo. From these early beginnings, came a toy which spanned both centuries and oceans.

In the 1700s, yo-yos became popular with European adults. In the 1960s, when Donald F. Duncan began manufacturing them in the United States, they quickly became a childhood sensation. It's estimated that there have been more than 1/2 billion yo-yos sold since 1930, and many of the early, wooden models are turning up in collections.

Among the most collectible are the wooden, mass-produced yo-yos dating from 1970 and earlier. The yo-yos made by Alox, Festival, Hasbro, and especially Duncan—the yo-yo king—are very collectible. These spinning toys sometimes show up at antique shows, flea markets and auctions. Prices are reasonable, ranging from a few dollars to about $50. Although all yo-yos basically do the same thing, there are a few variations to look for.

Over the years, yo-yos have been used as promotional gifts. Banks, appraisers, and other local businesses had these disks printed with their business names, logos, and addresses for advertising purposes.

Candy, cereal, and other products also used yo-yos in their marketing. These yo-yos appeal to both toy and advertising collectors. This means you can expect to pay considerably more for promotional yo-yos.

Other variations include yo-yos that spark, make music, light up, glow in the dark, and there are even some with cartoon characters on them. If, after an extensive search, you can't find any old yo-yos, you might want to go to a toy store to see what they have.

New plastic yo-yos also come in glow-in-the-dark, light-up, and musical models. And, while the plastic toys may not have the same appeal as the early wooden yo-yos, they can set you on the road to collecting. Expect to pay $5 or less for the new plastic toys. Also, look around in gift and specialty stores because you never know when a yo-yo will turn up.

The best way to display a yo-yo is to set it upright. Shelves, tables, and even cupboards can house a good-sized collection. If it's OK with your parents, you can also hang the yo-yos from the ceiling for an interesting display.

If you enjoy playing with yo-yos, then collecting these whirling discs is sure to make your head spin.

Related Collectibles: tops and other spinning toys